ANDY WARHOL'S
PARTY BOOK

text and photographs by
Andy Warhol and Pat Hackett

with
additional
photographs
by
Paige Powell,
Sam Bolton,
Wilfredo Rosado,
Jeffrey Slonim,
Edit de Ak,
and C.J. Zumwalt

Design by
Marc Balet

Crown Publishers, Inc. / New York

Published by Crown Publishers, Inc., 225 Park Avenue South, New York, New York, 10003 and represented in Canada by the Canadian MANDA Group.

CROWN is a trademark of Crown Publishers, Inc.

Manufactured in Japan

Library of Congress Cataloging-in-Publication Data

Warhol, Andy
  Andy Warhol's party book.

  1. Entertaining. I. Hackett, Pat. II. Title.
III. Title: party book.
GV1471.W265 1987   793.2   87-8837
ISBN 0-517-56698-2

10   9   8   7   6   5   4   3   2   1

First Edition

Andy died very unexpectedly in February 1987.
We had just finished this book and decided
to dedicate it . . .

To anyone who ever invited us anywhere
or didn't kick us out when we crashed.

P.H.
New York City
July 1988

Contents

Introduction: When You Care Enough to Come

Sex and parties are the two things that you still have to actually be there for—things that involve you and other people. For sex and parties, you still have to physically bring your lump of protoplasm and get it close to somebody else's. To carry on friendships or to cash checks or buy clothes, you can just make a phone call or send a computer message. To give court testimony or look for a date or read your own will after you're dead, you can send a videotape. To impregnate somebody and reproduce yourself, you can just send sperm.

Jerry Hall

You don't even have to be there to fight a war—you just send a bomb.

But for sex and parties, your body has to be there. The other people involved have to know that you cared enough to bring your body and get it reasonably close to theirs; that's the whole game. For example, when we watch the Academy Awards on TV, there are always some stars who can't be there personally because they're doing a play in London and they come on by satellite from their dressing rooms and say thank you, and we really hate them because they're not at the Dorothy Chandler Pavilion where they ought to be in order to entertain us better. Why should this matter to us, since we're not at either place (in the dressing room or at the awards ceremony)—we're just at home watching everybody on TV anyway? Because they didn't play the party game right—they didn't dress their body up in a dinner jacket or a gown and take it to the ceremony so we could feel excited that all the celebrities were together *in one place.*

The purest elements of a party are Time and Energy. You need a block of time that you designate as party time, and you need raw party energy. You need to let little things that would ordinarily bore you suddenly thrill you. You have to be willing to get happy about nothing. Say you're in the middle of a war at an army camp and there's going to be a party at seven P.M. (or 1900, since it's the army). Well, at seven everyone looks at their watch and agrees, "Now it's time. Now we're different people." You don't need drinks or drugs—you just need a watch. You then forget about the bad things and think about the good things because this is the time you've set aside for that.

It's all in your attitude. If there were five dull people in a room having a party it would be boring, but if something extra happened to excite them—for example, if they knew that somebody was outside waiting to kill them—it wouldn't be so boring. The important thing is to infuse everything with as much drama as you can. A dull person is someone who asks you, "Will the party be amusing?" because you know that that person is going to want to *be* amused, rather than be amusing. A great party person is someone who's looking for a new place to *be* fun, not just *have* fun.

Parties should have a feeling of a-part-ness—they should be different from the rest of your life, they should make it more special. In Manhattan, where people live in *apart*-ments, a part-y makes them feel like they're *a part* of something.

Big smiles make a party better because they're energy. I like the kind of people who stride over to you with their hand out and say, "Hi! I'm Bill Johnson!" You want to have these key extroverts at any party to kick things along. (But there's no way to tell in advance who a good guest or a bad guest will be, because someone can be a really fun person but be really dull that night or in a bad mood, and maybe someone you thought would never have anything interesting to say can turn out to be the life of the party. You never know until the next morning, when you're running through what happened the night before, doing a postmortem of the party, a post-partum.)

"Hypocritical" only applies to personal relationships, not to party deportment. At a party you just have to be fun, you don't have to be honest. However, some people push this too far. Take, for example, the Japanese. When you go to parties in Japan at the end of a work-day, the Japanese turn into different people after a few drinks. They let their hair down and get wild and promise anything and say anything because everybody who's Japanese, I guess, knows that it doesn't count, that the next day nobody expects anybody to be accountable for anything he said or did at the party. But I think it's pathetic to commit yourself to something and then not do it. Why get in over your head? The next time you see the person, you'll have to crawl into the corner and think, I said I was going to send him that photograph and I never did. . . . But the Japanese don't seem to mind—as long as they're at a party, they'll tell you they're going to send you a *billion* photographs.

I asked Lionel Tiger, a social anthropologist who lives here in Manhattan, about hypocrisy, along with other party-related issues, and here are his thoughts:

What's the purpose of a party?

In big cities like New York the party is essentially a mechanism for bringing together people who wouldn't otherwise be together, such as a wrestler and a sculptor. In smaller communities like, say, an army base, the party is an opportunity for the same people who are always together to be together *again,* but under different circumstances.

So with a party you're either creating a new scene or raising the excitement level of your regular scene.

Right. In metropolitan areas you heighten your existing social structure rather than create another one. Remember, 39 percent of the people in Manhattan are living alone. Astonishing. So the party provides some sort of connecting tissue. People have always had parties—whether they're "after work" parties or "after harvest" parties—frequently accompanied by alcohol or dances or ceremonies. But what were places like Studio 54 or Area if not a ceremony? And what is Nell's? You have to have the right costume, know the right social formula, and there are always the keepers of the sacred flame outside the doors of these places deciding who'll gain entry. . . . So primitive cultures are not that different from ours.

Why do people go to parties?

For people under the age of twenty-five or thirty, a party has a sexual-allocation function. It allows them to make new friends, to assess their own sexuality, and to compare their partners with others. This function doesn't end completely at thirty—it continues to apply throughout the adult cycle in, for example, places that breed adultery, such as country clubs. But for people over thirty, parties mainly become a status-affirming function; they give people the feeling that they must be rather significant, since here are these other significant people all around them. And a

Pat Hackett and Andy Warhol on New Year's Eve

Early Madonna with record producer
Jelly Bean Benitez

party gives people the chance to understand their world in more personal terms—they may meet a Procter or a Gamble or someone who works for the Met, and once they've met an actual person, a world that was before totally anonymous and abstract becomes concrete and real. People like to be at a party with important people because it makes them feel important—part of the world, rather than excluded from it. At these status-affirming events, there has to be status equivalence; that is, you can't ask someone who's really out of it.

Should you be sincere or phony at parties?

Sincerity is a vastly overrated hormone. People are sincere being a little insincere. It's like trying to determine authenticity and you end up in the middle of Africa somewhere; it's a false premise. For some people the kind of aggressive insincerity of glad-handing is as important a feature of going to a party as talking to their dog is when they're at home. So I suspect that it's more wholesome and more robust to assume that everybody at a party is really being what they are *under those circumstances.* It's a very partial part of life. By definition, it's just a party, just an episode.

What are the elements of a good party?

You have to look at the party as a kind of four-hour drama where everybody has an appointed role. You get certain people who're always supposed to be entertaining—they're witty or they're sharp or they're nasty—and there are others who are supposed to be charming or "have secrets," and there are other people who are expected to give sexual gossip, etc. People get typecast for parties just as they do in the theater or movies.

What does a party mean to the person who's giving it?

You intensify your sense of your own existence by creating a kaleidoscopic version of your whole life—you choose one friend from here,

one friend from there. You're not putting people under a microscope—on the contrary, you're amplifying them.

Have the topics of conversation changed much in the last twenty-five years?

Conversations about such personal things as, say, orifices used to be impossible, but now they're acceptable because people are very concerned with self-management and will talk about their lives almost as if they were talking about business enterprises. Therefore it's important for them to find out from other people how *they* treat specific personal problems. This is also a reflection of increased loneliness—

because so many people in New York live alone, they really have no one to talk to about, say, bad breath, so at parties they now raise topics that would once have been purely domestic issues.

How many people does it take to make a party?

Obviously the minimum in order to have a real sense of party is three. Four is better because it creates enough uncertainty about what's going to be said. You need that surprising, dramatic element. If it were only two people, you would still be in control; it's just a dialogue. With three you don't know for sure—there's slight drama—but with four, then it's out of your

hands totally, so it's a party.

When is a party successful?

When people wish they could repeat it the next day.

I've been to thousands and thousands of parties in my life. I don't have those beautiful social graces so I'm not the greatest guest and I'm certainly not the greatest host, either, since I don't know how to make people feel (a) comfortable or (b) uncomfortable in an exciting way. (More later on the qualities of good hosts and hostesses.) But over the years I've had some thoughts about what goes on when people decide to have a party or go to one.

11

Grace Jones

How to Get Fun Out of a Good Time

I like to have a receiving line at parties. It's not just a tedious exercise you go through at a formal occasion—it has a purpose, and I think it would be great if less formal events started using them. Everybody you're supposed to meet at the party is right there in the line, and you have someone there to hype you to them: "This is Andy Warhol. He does those wonderful paintings and publishes that marvelous magazine, *Interview,* and films those fabulous music videos." That way later on when you want to go talk to someone, you don't have

Artist Kenny Scharf

to find somebody to introduce you. You can just go up and say, "Remember me? I just met you in the line."

Usually, though, you're just going to a party because you want to see all the people there, so I think a great party would start with a line comprised of just the guest of honor and someone to tell him or her who everyone is. Then as people came in, they'd go down the line shaking hands and then add themselves to the end of the line so that the line would just keep growing, and by the end of the party everybody would have seen and shaken hands with everybody else. And you could even dance in the line while you were shaking hands.

Or, another good party would be one where the whole thing was just one big receiving line that would stretch from the entrance to the exit, and you'd check your coat and go down the line and they'd have your coat ready for you at the exit door as you left. That way you'd know right away what kind of a party you've been at, and you wouldn't have to wait until the next day to find out who you missed who was hiding in the shadows.

I've finally learned not to do long, elaborate introductions—the kind where you tell too much about a person so there's nothing left for the other person to ask. It's something most people already know, but I did it for years and it was awful. I'd say things like, "This is Jane and her father likes black men and her mother had a facelift and she just graduated from Brown and she goes to AA every day and she's just the girl for you because she'll boss you around and you like that." Instead you should say just enough to get people slightly interested. If, for example, a man likes fat women, say, "This is Tom, he's a chubby chaser." Period. And that will get them talking, even if it's only to deny it or say how rude you are.

If you don't remember two people's names and so you can't introduce them, just heave a big sigh and say, "Oh, I'm so tired of introducing people, I've been doing it all night—why don't you just introduce yourselves?"

Valentino, Jonathan Lieberson, Kitty Hawks, and Diane von Furstenberg

Carmen de Lavallade, Cornelia Guest, and Geoffrey Holder

Photographer Patrick McMullan and Laurie Ogle

When you find yourself in a conversation with somebody and you don't remember their name, you're waiting for that one clue that's going to answer the question, "Who is this person and what did he have to do with my life?" But frankly, not knowing people's names doesn't bother me. I've had major conversations with people without knowing their names. It's not an issue unless they decide to make it one. Usually you're just out, meeting interesting new people, and you're not talking about anything important. It's just of-the-moment. When you'd be standing in the middle of the Mike Todd Room at the Palladium talking to someone, the odds were you weren't making a lifelong friend—you were making a "Mike Todd friend." "Nice to see you, we had a nice talk, got a little too drunk, said a little too much, but that was nice, bye-bye now . . ." Relax. At a certain level, names aren't important.

And you shouldn't use last names much, anyway. Just first names. If people want to know last names, they'll get to the point where they just ask each other. Don't load them down prematurely with useless information. I personally hate it when people call me "Mr. Warhol." It makes you feel old and bureaucratized. If I pick up the phone and someone asks for "Mr. Warhol," that's it, I hang up, because who is it going to be but someone you don't want to talk to? It's like opening mail. Mail is trouble. People are not out there writing you checks. Friends you talk to on the phone. Mail is from people who call you "Mr." Okay, fine, if it's an airline and they're calling to say that they got you into nonsmoking—I don't need for an airline to call me "Andy"—but otherwise it's too depressing to be reminded all the time that you're past the age of thirteen. People could say that calling you "Mr." is just a sign of respect, but that's not true; I find I get much more respect from the people who call me "Andy."

For instance, I went to the seventy-fifth anniversary of the Oreo cookie not long ago. I'd gotten a letter inviting me and I

RSVPed right away because I hoped it would lead to a commission from Nabisco to do a portrait of the cookie, which is really beautiful. So I arrive at the Waldorf Astoria all dressed in black and white for the occasion, and I'm walking toward the banquet room when I hear, "Oh, Mr. Warhol?" and I turn around and it's a man walking toward me. I think, "Gee, great. He recognizes me and he's coming to take me to some VIP area where the cookie is." But no, this guy was Security and what he wanted to know was, "Are you crashing, Mr. Warhol?" The PR lady had to come over and tell him it was okay to let me go in. So "Mr." is not really a sign of respect; it usually just means that trouble's on the way.

That incident reminds me of another point: There's no nice way to ask a person at a party if he was actually invited. Once you question someone inside the party, you break the party mood. Yvon Dihe, once a French film actor and now a PR man in New York, has a smooth, charming way to find out if a guest at a party has been invited without offending them by asking: He sends a photographer over to take their picture, and then tells them he needs to know how to spell their name in case they use the picture in the newspapers. Then he just checks the guest list to see if the person is on it.

Some people say that a good party is when you never do find out anybody's last name or what kind of a job he has. Unfortunately, a group that really loves a party like this is the IRS, because those parties are not at all deductible.

True parties and true love are similar: With true love, you get nothing out of it but love, and with true parties, you get nothing out of them but fun. But nowadays with the tax laws the way they are, the government forces you to talk business at parties. And when one person takes out a business card, suddenly everybody else starts pulling *theirs* out. And when you get home you have lots of cards and you can't remember the faces that go with them. I suggest creating a new kind of business card called Party

Decorator Jed Johnson at the annual Polo Ball in Greenwich, Connecticut

Cards, where it's a photo of you on one side and then whatever information you want to put on the other side. Even actors and actresses could do away with all those big eight-by-ten glossies that they go around with. It would be so much more subtle to hand somebody this small size. It wouldn't matter if you were a businessman or a glamour-puss—the uses are limitless when you combine a photo with a business card. Kids could even use them at the beach. Almost like baseball cards. Party Cards. For dating and careering.

Every guest owes it to the host or hostess to make as much conversation as he can. The type and extent of the talk varies with the type of party. At a sit-down dinner party, "turning the table" isn't as strict as it used to be, it just happens sort of naturally and you make sure you talk to both sides of you. Sometimes when you're in a secure mood and you're between two people who're talking to their other sides, it feels so great to be off the hook and just stare into space because they've forgotten about you. But then other times, if you're feeling blue and the people next to you keep talking to their other partners, you feel so unappreciated and you think, "What has my life been for?" And you just sit there and you're not even hungry and you try to be happy but here are two people who've found others they like so much better than you on the other sides of them. It's humiliating. I've noticed that some men push their chair back just a little bit from the table, so they can talk to the ladies on both sides of them at the same time when one lady has been left hanging by her other partner, and that's a kind, casual technique that works well.

Some people are better at conversation than others. Kids who grew up in rich families where they got sent to things like dancing classes seem to have more social graces than most of us. My friend Franco Rosselini is an international dinner party pro: "I can talk to a wall," he assures me. "To, a, wall. And I do it with pleasure, because it comes so easily to me. It's an at-

Lady Neidpath, the former Catherine Guinness, in the dining room at Stanway House, Gloucestershire

titude you have if you like to keep yourself surrounded by people. Because you go to these seated dinners and you're suddenly sitting next to God knows who, and if they have nothing to say, that's fine, I will speak all by myself. This is why they invite me. Sometimes worse than silence is when one of these walls asks me something foolish like what do I do for a living. What can I tell them? 'Nothing.' The truth."

When you're having trouble talking to somebody you don't seem to have anything in common with, you can sometimes get lucky and hit on something. I once asked someone I couldn't think of anything to say to if she'd seen the azaleas in the park that week, and she went into ecstasies and gave me a dissertation on azaleas for an hour and it was sort of interesting.

Sometimes worse than having adults get bored with you is watching kids just yawn in your face. One night I was at Yoko Ono's and Sean was being friendly, but I could see he was really bored. It's not easy to thrill a ten-year-old. The artist Jay Shriver was with me, and he got inspired to tell Sean the secret of how you tear a phone book in half—you bake it in the oven until it gets dry and then it's easy. Then I got inspired and told Sean that if he was bored, why didn't he learn how to read the phone book. I asked him if he knew who the first person in the phone book was, or the last one. He started to get interested, so we got the Manhattan directory out and he called Information and asked for the number of the AAAAAAAA Bar and Grill, and the operator said, "Yes, sir, the AAAAAAAA Bar and Grill." And then we called back and asked for Richard M. Nixon's number and she said, "Wait a minute, sir," and we could hear a click like they were tracing us and Sean got scared and hung up, and then I got him more scared by telling him that just because you hang up a phone doesn't mean it's really hung up—that they could still find you. Then we dialed F-U-C-K-Y-O-U and L-O-V-E-Y-O-U just to see what would happen, and then Yoko and her friend Sam Havadtoy dialed the White

Artist James Mathers

House and a recording said that if you wanted to talk to President Reagan to call back between one and five in the afternoon. We had so much fun just because we found a prop. As I said, you can get lucky.

In the old days of strict Emily Post etiquette, you weren't supposed to talk about things like business and diseases and politics and religion in social situations, but now everybody seems to. And emotions go in and out of style, too. In the days before sixty-six when people would get embarrassed easily, it was great to find people who said shocking things and just didn't care—"shame" was out. But today, when hardly anything embarrasses anybody, it's kind of refreshing to find a person who still blushes and realizes when they should be ashamed.

People are always asking, "How can I get away from a dull person at a party?" I don't really know, because I'm never able to do it. Sometimes I do get rescued, but it's usually by another dull person. When they're trying to get away from you, people usually say they have to go to the bathroom or get a drink or make a phone call. The writer Steven M. L. Aronson has an ingenious technique. He always carries two drinks so that if he wants to get away from you he tells you that he was on his way to deliver the other drink to someone on the other side of the room. But the only problem with that trick, he says, is that if everybody used it, you'd have a room full of people with drinks in both hands and all of them running away from each other. A party running away from itself.

There are occasions when you don't want people to talk to you. Here's one: This man was making small talk with me and a few other people at a cocktail party. I asked him, "What do you do?" He said, "I work for Sylvester Stallone's

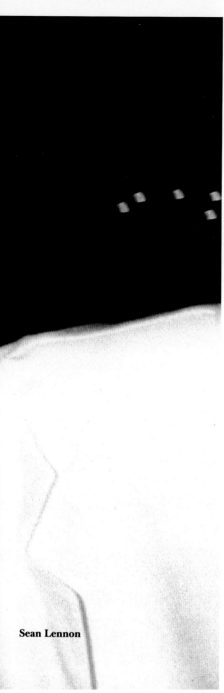

Sean Lennon

tually go out and buy their own dinner jacket. Before that it's usually thrift-shop fare and rentals. I'm like most men in that I don't like having to put on black tie. I hate ties, I hate collars that button, I hate French cuffs—I hate everything about a tuxedo except that I happen to know it makes me look fabulous. In fact, dinner jackets make every man look terrific because they're a uniform and you can't beat a uniform for glamour. I never wore one at all except for a few years in the Seventies when I got tired of being underdressed everywhere I went and I just decided to wear a tuxedo day and night so I wouldn't have that intimidated feeling that you get when you're constantly underdressed when everybody else looks sensational. But I found that I was still intimidated whether I was dressed right or not, because when I did dress to the hilt, I found that I was intimidated by my own clothes. They felt like they were too much for me. I didn't know if I was worthy of them. I didn't feel relaxed and in control of the situation. So by wearing a dinner jacket all day and night—under leather jackets, with jeans, to the coffee shop, and walking the dog—I got over feeling intimidated by the idea that I was dressed up, and after that, no matter what the occasion, I was fine.

However, I'm one of those people who can never look perfect—the bow tie's always tilting. I walk by a mirror and there it is, practically vertical. Now, though, I don't even wear the tie—I just wear turtlenecks. I got that from Halston, the turtleneck look (although he does wear ties, too). And I'll never be a person who can wear white shirts. I look down and there's something *on* it and it's not white anymore.

Not all men dislike getting dressed up, though—some really love it. There's an opera club that's men only and they go every week to the opera in black tie and to dinner afterwards. Very committed opera lovers. A lot of traditions like this are carried on because some young man arrives in New York and he's working for a bank, and maybe his senior officer has an interest like this and he thinks that having it,

too, will advance him, which it probably will. And I was talking to a stockbroker named Alan Feuer once who said he was truly happy only when he was formally dressed. He owned not only his own black tie, but his own white tie, too, and his greatest pleasure was going to every one of the big charity balls so he could dance all night with women in beautiful gowns. Walking home from a ball at six o'clock in the morning across Central Park, in tails and a top hat, was his idea of heaven. I asked him, though, if he had many friends who felt the same way and he said, "No. I'm shocked at how alone I am in this."

In a way, though, I like going to a party in the clothes I've worn all day, because then you're not putting pressure on your host or hostess, like you're expecting them to make something really great happen and so you dressed up for it. If you look a little bedraggled, they can feel that *anything* they do for you is going to make you feel better—even just getting you a cold glass of water—that it doesn't have to be something spectacular.

Formal parties seem like they go back to Old World days—they certainly didn't develop on the frontier. They're throwbacks, probably, to Europe and Mozart and that style of elegance. For most people, this is a real party, because it takes them out of the ordinary world and puts them into something they think of as "special."

If you have several places to go in the same night, the best thing to do is follow the advice of the fashion designer Larissa and "Dress for the most dressy one and never feel embarrassed that you're overdressed at the other places." I asked her how she had the energy to go out everynight and she said, "But I don't! People *think* I go out all the time and it's not true. What happens is, when I do go out once every three weeks, I wear some spectacular lamé thing, maybe, and it makes an impression on people so they think I'm constantly out on the town; you see, if I wore some little housecoat no one would notice me. But when I go out, I go *all* the way out."

Some women manage to change

mother." I said, "Oh, really? What business are you in?" He said, "The same she's in—skin peeling." I said, "You help her peel the skin?" He said, "Oh, no. I'm a salesman. What I do is, I get invited to parties like this and when I see people with bad skin I talk to them and give them her card." There was a stunned silence as he reached into his pocket and then we all screamed, "Oh, my God! Why are you talking to *us?*" It's a funny idea, though. I wonder if Stallone calls people up and says, "My mother's got this guy needs some parties to go to."

In asking around I found that thirty is the age when most men ac-

Fashion designer Azzedine Alaïa with
Tina Chow

their whole look as the evening
moves along. I remember being out
one night with Tina Chow and at
the formal dinner party we went to
first, she wore a beautiful Fortuny
dress, and then when we left there
to go downtown to Area, she peeled
the dress off in the car, twisted it
around her neck, and went dancing
in her black body stocking and this
"scarf."

To have a really good time, you
don't have to actually look good,
you just have to *think* that you do. If
you can convince yourself that you
look fabulous, you can save yourself
the trouble of primping. But then,
of course, if you skip primping, you
lose the side benefits. The whole
physical process of getting yourself
ready for a party is also a way of pre-
paring for it mentally. Grooming
yourself puts you in the party
mood. If you think you look good,
you're going to be more willing to
believe that other people like you,
and that's all-important. You have
to walk into that room feeling popular. A true party person, if he wins
the Lottery, will get a limousine before he gets an apartment. Parties
are a forum for your popularity,
real or imagined. And as everybody
knows, you always do attract the
treatment that you think you
deserve.

To get the most glamour out of a
party, you shouldn't go into it cold.
It's like if you have a big meeting on
Wall Street, you're not going to ride
down on a dirty subway—or even in
a bouncing cab—and then try to
scrape the gum off your shoes before you walk in. Nobody gets rich
that way. You don't walk in like a
bum off the street. Same thing
when you go to a big party. You
can't change your life in a moment
right as you get to the doorway the
way impressionists can when they
turn their back to the audience and
then face them as a new person.
Most of us need a little preparation
to get into the mood we need. You
need to go down in a car with good
shocks, one that's comfortable, air
conditioned, and well-driven—by
somebody else. Most times you
don't need, necessarily, a stretch
limo with a bar and a phone, because that can be pretty pimpy, but

then sometimes feeling flashy like a pimp may be just what you *do* want—it depends on your mood. The important thing is to create a little "pocket of elegance," a comfortable fantasy that you can slip into for a few hours. In other words, *wasting money* puts you in a real party mood—throwing it away on tips, letting it fall out of your jacket and not bothering to pick it up, ordering more of something than you could ever need—all this gives you the expansive, popular feeling you do need in order to face people and have fun.

When to arrive? I like early. I'm beyond worrying about Fashionably Late. (And I think everybody else is, too, because with population growth what it is today, most people have found that being fashionably late can mean that there physically won't be any room left for you. More on that when we talk about clubs and openings.) One dividend of being the first one there is that all the people arriving after you think you're *giving* the party and they thank you for inviting them. Also, if you're shy, you go crazy if you have to walk into a room with a hundred people and you don't know who to look at first and you feel like you're making faux pas all over the place and you end up being rude to everybody. Whereas when you're there early, you can meet people one by one as they arrive, which is nice. And you can really get a good look at the flowers before the crush starts.

Another reason for getting there first is to eat before the food gets messed up and before people start coming up to you and kissing you while you have carrots stuck in your teeth and chopped-liver breath. Get all of that over with early. I panic when I get there at the height of a party: Where's a good place to sit? Who do I know here? What's the food? Did I miss any good hors d'oeuvres? How many bars are there? I mean sometimes you can't see over other people's heads. I get a nervous breakdown from that. When you get there early, you can scout everything out and know exactly where you stand.

In the case of a sit-down dinner,

Larissa

though, it's important to know your hostess's M.O. Maybe from experience you know that she invites people for eight-thirty but never serves dinner before ten, so in that case you arrive at maybe nine-fifteen so you don't have to stand around drinking for an hour and a half.

I like John Sex's attitude. He told me, "I always arrive on time, which is early because parties never start 'on time.' If the party starts at twelve, I'm all ready by eleven-thirty, I leave my house at eleven forty-five, and when I get there—at twelve on the dot—they're usually still getting things together. Then I sit around and watch the party start, and a lot of times I'm also the last one to leave. I really wring it out."

There are two kinds of great hosts and hostesses, and this goes for restaurants and clubs as well as parties. First there are the kind that are always beaming and wonderful, and you like to go to their places be-cause they make *you* beam and feel wonderful and comfortable. And next there are the kind who're split personalities, who are so nice to you one time and just ignore you the next. Or maybe even they get mean. With these people, you go to their places for the drama—waiting to see if they'll be horrible to you or not. This is like high school, when you didn't know if somebody would be your friend this week or not. No matter how old they get, nobody ever completely loses this mentality, so the hosts who flip out and scream at their guests every so often put a little drama in your life, and this type always then makes up for it by being extra *extra* generous the next time. Anyway, it all evens out with the ones who are extra gener-ous consistently. It just depends on your mood, which type you feel like being with on a given night. Comfort or drama, take your pick.

The art collector Stuart Pivar gave me an interesting insight as to why certain people become hosts. In his apartment off Central Park West, Stuart gives musicales where virtuoso musician friends of his like pianist Christopher O'Riley play great music all evening. Friends wander in and out. It's very infor-mal, and it's the closest thing I can imagine to the old salons of Europe where artists and writers would sit around and plot cultural and politi-cal revolutions. Stuart has filled his place with magnificent works of art mainly from the eighteenth and nineteenth centuries, and with an-tique musical instruments. The furniture is plush and the piano is draped with ancient pieces of cloth. All in all, it looks like the perfect setting for some rich nineteenth-century rake to despoil young vir-gins in. Stuart's a relaxed host, and when I asked him what inspired him to do all this for his friends week after week, he explained, "I'm a host for one simple reason: I hate to go out. Even when I was a child, I couldn't wait for rainy days because then I'd get to stay in. If I didn't

Bianca and Alana

Pianist Christopher O'Riley about to perform at Stuart Pivar's "salon"

have these musicales where people come over to my place, I'd never see anybody." So this is a quality common to many hosts, I guess—they're not restless, they don't mind being the ones who aren't on the move.

The entrance to a party area is really important, because it gets you into a specific frame of mind right off. Newspaper columnist and mycologist (mushroom expert) Maryetta Devereaux, out in Portland, Oregon, used to give dinner parties in a family-size teepee beside her beachhouse. She'd cook dinner in the center pit and everyone would sit around Indian-style. She noticed that no matter how formal someone's attitude was when he got to the house, that after he had to crouch down to go in through the flapped entrance, he immediately got a better attitude.

People like to give parties when their apartments or houses are completely finished being decorated. However, I love parties in half-finished places—I don't like anything ever to be finished, and a place always has more atmosphere when it's under construction than when it's all done. Sharon McCluskey Sondes gave a party *while*

her apartment was being redecorated and it was great, very Venetian-like with everything decayed-looking and falling down around you. There was no electricity, so she used candles, and the walls were in various stages of being peeled down from the fifteenth to the sixth coat of paint and it was great.

Every little thing you buy for a party costs a staggering amount, so when you see a whole mass of anything, you've really got to give people credit. I always notice flowers. As soon as you see flowers, you know the hosts have spent big money, because you know how expensive the simplest little pot of petunias is that you send your cousin in Cleveland who's just had a baby. These mammoth arrangements let you know you're in the middle of beauty bought by big bucks.

Renny Reynolds is a party designer who got into that business through first being a florist, so he's very conscious of getting the right *kind* of flowers—the right size and shape—for each specific place. He says, "In a huge space, flowers alone can't give a place a 'look' because they tend to get lost. I've seen some party designers try to bank the cor-

ners of the promenade of the State Theater at Lincoln Center—a huge, cold, four-story space—with eighteen-foot trees, and it doesn't work. You have to have things there that really take over the space. For instance, one year there we did umbrella forms coming down at the center of each table that were covered with smilax vines, so that it looked like everyone was sitting under a Victorian gazebo that was growing and had orchids dripping off it and candles suspended from it. *That* dominated the space."

George Trescher, a planner who's worked on events ranging from the Literary Lions Dinner to Caroline Kennedy's wedding, agrees: "It's all scale—to make your statement and make it dramatic but not pretentious."

When you have flowers at home, you should have someone come to the house to do them in your own vases and things, because "arrangements" from florists look awful. Make it look normal.

Twenty minutes after any party starts, you can't smell the flowers anymore—it's all just perfume and cigarette smoke—so again, just to smell, it's good to be early. I always wonder what it feels like to the

flower petals to have to fend off all that cigarette smoke, because you know how awful your skin starts to feel in a really smoked-up room. (Incidentally, I refresh myself at parties by taking out of my bag one of those plastic spray bottles that you mist your plants with and giving my face a few good, long squirts of water; this helps counteract that smokehouse feeling.) I asked florist Robert Isabell if he thought the flowers had a hard time at parties, and he said, "No, they just keep breathing and the smoke doesn't stick to them the way it does to clothes." When he was eight years old, Robert started working in greenhouses in Minnesota. Years later he moved to New York and put that experience together with lighting and decoration and became a party designer. I wondered what the stages were in a career as a florist, so I asked him, "What was your first big break? What was the job that really made you?" He thought for a minute and then said, "It doesn't work that way with flowers."

People are really split on whether food is everything at a party or nothing. To people like your relatives, it seems to mean a lot—that's all they talk about when you ask them how a party was; they'll just tell you about the food in detail. But then kids who go around to all the parties every night don't care about the food at all—they just care about who was there and if the music was good, things like that. I do something really rude at parties, though. When I see one bowl of something that I really like, I'll stand right in front of it and eat that one thing until I wipe it off the face of the table. Like if there's giant strawberries, I'll just stand there and eat one after the other. Or caviar. I went to a caviar-tasting party at Cartier's last year and this one kind tasted so good that I just planted myself in front of it and ate and ate and ate. You know, when they're serving caviar they have these tiny little spoons and these mini-pieces of toast all laid out so that you'll get the hint that you're supposed to take these little blueberry-size servings. Well, forget it. I just shoveled it into my mouth. My only regret was that I didn't have an ice-cream scooper in my pocket. I got embarrassed finally when this lady who'd been up there serving herself about fifteen minutes before came back and saw me still there, holding my station, so I lied. I said, "I went away to make a phone call, then I came back." Now, what I did was greedy, but frankly I just didn't care; when you focus in on one particular food, you lose your perspective. I only stop when I'm full.

When I see cold shellfish—like shrimp and clams—that says to me that somebody really went all out. Someone carving a fresh ham is very nice, and those dishes of stainless steel with curry in them are always lovely, you see a lot of those, and aspics are attractive, but it's the cold shellfish and smoked salmon that tell you this cost important money.

In New York, a lot of the waiters and waitresses, especially those who work with caterers, are in the theater and movie business, or they're models, and they're always much more beautiful than the people they're waiting on. So while they're "serving," they're able to say to themselves, "I'll get my big break and I'll be on film soon." So that's a very different thing from the permanent servants like in *Upstairs, Downstairs*, where it's their whole lot in life. True, these people *could* end up doing this for the rest of their lives, but theoretically, they don't have to.

It always sounds weird and pretentious when an American says, "the servants." It's okay to say, "How many do you have serving?" or to use the specific job titles—waiters or bartenders or cooks, or just "the help." Americans do, of course, have servants, but more often they just get around the problem by subcontracting out—hiring caterers and bartenders for specific occasions.

Designer Stephen Sprouse

Debbie Harry

Tom Cashin told me that Serge at Glorious Food gives a four-hour seminar once a month to all would-be waiters and waitresses to indoctrinate them with the Glorious philosophy, so I called up and reserved a space. . . .

WAITER EMERITUS

Handsome Serge De Cluny was also a model for ten years. He started as a waiter for a famous caterer, Donald Bruce White, and then he was in charge of the executive dining room at CBS for a while. When Glorious Food asked him to work for them, to be a captain and to conduct seminars for new waiters, he called in even the waiters who were already working there and he reeducated them. He told me, "Every Glorious Food waiter has to realize that we are something special. In the seminars I teach them how to wait, but most important, I give them spirit." When I made a reference to the days when he used to be a waiter himself, he corrected me: "I am still a waiter. Absolutely. I don't want to lose that contact. I want to do everything before Madam asks—that's the little game I play in my mind. If she thinks of something before I do, I lose my game."

Here are a few things Serge tells the new recruits:

The staff

"Today, people don't have big staffs, so we are replacing the butlers—we are playing their staff. For this reason, especially, it's very important when you arrive at a house to find out where the bathrooms are, because if you don't know, that can really give you away when a guest asks you, 'Where's the bathroom?' If you go, 'Uhhh, gee . . .' you are obviously not 'from the house'. . . .

"There are no unimportant positions. If I put you on coats and you have an expression on your face like you don't want to be there, it's going to look like they hired the guy next door for ten bucks. . . .

"For serving, the general rule is we start with the woman—even when President Reagan is there, because he is a gallant man. Although when we had Prince Rainier, he inisted on being served first. . . .

"Now, being pushy and being attentionate are two different things.

28

Party attendants

Being attentionate is worth a fortune nowadays, because it's rare. To notice what people need, to remember what they like and what they don't, these are nice touches and you are going to feel so good when you do these things, I guarantee it. Memory, as they say, is a question of interest. . . .

"Usually, you put three ashtrays down for a table of ten. Sometimes the hostess will say don't put them down until dessert. But not if Mrs. Kissinger is coming, because she smokes from the time she arrives until she leaves, and the purpose of etiquette is to make everybody feel comfortable. . . .

"As a rule, you will refuse tips. An exception is when a person specifically wants to let you know how much he appreciates something you've done. In that case, because it's obvious he knows he doesn't have to, you can accept the tip. . . .

SERVICE AND ATTITUDE

Tom Cashin and Jay Johnson are both working models and waiters right now. Tom's also an Irish step dancer who was in The Best Little Whorehouse in Texas *when it was on Broadway, and he works in off-Broadway shows and TV commercials. I asked them:*

How come the male waiters are usually all knockout beauties?

TC: Most caterers prefer good-looking guys, because really good-looking girls would be competition for the hostesses—all the men would be talking to them when they went around with the hors d'oeuvres. But actually, they talk to a lot of the guys, too, just to find out what they do besides "this." Actors, models, opera singers, dancers. That's when the eight-by-ten glossies come out. I always carry them.

Have you ever gotten an acting job because of a party you'd waited at?

TC: I've gotten auditions. But usually they just want you to work at a party of *theirs.* You know, "I'm having this great party and I want you to be there" *(laughs).* To wait. But a couple of times they've invited me to their parties just as a guest.

Do you ever feel embarrassed serving people?

JJ: I used to feel uncomfortable, but now I think it doesn't matter, that it's money I can pay my bills with, and that's what really matters. I'm happy.

What about when you've had to serve people you know socially?

TC: Yeah, you do feel funny. I was working at this wedding out in the Hamptons, and it turned out the bride was a model I knew—I'd done a shoot with her for *Mademoiselle.* She saw me and said, "Tom?? What're *you* doing here?" And I said, "I'm working with the caterer today." She said, "Oh, isn't that great?"

And I said *(laughs),* "Yeah, isn't it?" She introduced me to her mother and everything, and I was ready to throw myself into the Atlantic Ocean. It happens all the time, because in New York everything's so close, elbow to elbow, you're constantly running into everybody. But I remind myelf of the actors who used to work for Glorious Food who're on TV now and making movies. Very few of the waiters don't have other careers. But if you wanted to, you could work ten parties a week, because they have all these executive lunches up at Paine Webber and Dillon Reed, and all these kinds of Madison Avenue–type places. I only do a couple a week because I have a Polaroid commercial running now.

What kinds of things make your job harder?

TC: If there's a theme for the party and you have to wear crazy outfits. Although I had to wear a top hat and tails once, and I didn't mind that. But that time I wasn't waiting—they'd picked me and another tall waiter to greet the guests at the door. And another thing is the kind of hostesses who breathe down your neck every minute—you're never quick enough, you're never good enough—and who talk mean to the help. Sometimes you'll work at a party where they've spent so much money on everything—the best champagne, the best food—and then they don't tip you. It's surprising.

What's the usual ratio of waiters to guests?

TC: If they're really doing it up, they'll hire a lot. Like if it's a dinner for eighteen, they'll get at least three or four guys, and that's in addition to the cook and the kitchen people. Now I work for some Swedish girls downtown. I used to work for Glorious, but they were so serious about everything. Sean Driscoll started the company years ago—he used to be an Irish step dancer, like me.

Serge of Glorious Food

"Sometimes people will ask you something very obvious and you'll think they're making fun of you. They'll point at a piece of chicken and say, 'What is that?' They're not putting you on—they can't see! I know one socialite who likes me to very discreetly point to everything and whisper to her, 'This is veal, this is tomatoes, this is caviar,' because she is not seeing. It's our little secret. . . .

"When I first began to serve, I had to manipulate my mind to think, How can I get some value out of this experience? Let me share with you some of these manipulations. . . . Ego is your worst enemy. There's always a smart way to handle people who are giving you trouble—you behave with class. That way you will never lose. . . . When someone is giving a dinner or a wedding or a bar mitzvah or a birthday party, this is a special time for them, and as you perform that night, you become part of that person's life forever—you are in their history. Sometimes when I look up and see our lines marching in, holding those trays of spun-sugar desserts up high—sometimes it seems like those trays are just floating in on air, and I tell you, it gives me chills. There's more to being a Glorious Food waiter than service—we give a *production!* We rise to *every* occasion!"

Serge's seminar was persuasive— he's charming and there can't possibly be anyone in the world who's better at what he does. But I have to admit that when we had to get up and practice with the dishes and the silverware, the physical act of "serving" actually did unnerve me. I'd gone in thinking, Gee, what a great way to make extra money. But seeing how you'd have to keep your mouth shut and always be beneath the party guests— somehow I have to admit that this did bother me. But then I had a revelation. I thought, Well, no wonder so many waiters are actors—this is all just *acting.* Most waiters and waitresses in America can get out of waiting anytime, if they want, so they must be doing it because they *choose* to. Waiters are just actors *acting* like servants so

Paige Powell with Sirio Maccioni of Le Cirque

Actor/model/waiter Tom Cashin

Steven Greenberg and *A Chorus Line* star Donna McKechnie

that guests can feel "served." As a waiter, you just have to realize: I'm allowing them to think that I'm their servant. Let them enjoy it while they can, because it's only going to last a few hours, and they won't get it again until my next performance. While I'm performing, though, I'm going to be good.

I learned something interesting from a waiter at a dinner I went to a few months ago: The food you *see* displayed is not always what you're being served. There was a Smithfield ham out on the table, but the waiter said that in the kitchen the hostess was having the help cut up boiled ham and that that's what the guests were really being served. So then I wondered what that big, beautiful, expensive ham was doing there. Had she rented it? Was this a rented ham on tour going from party to party? Or did they own it, and were they waiting for a better party to serve it at? Or were they just going to eat it themselves some night when they were home alone? I guess I'll never know.

I asked Truman Capote at lunch one afternoon if he was going to a particular party later on that night, and he growled, "Why should I? I can *drink* at home." But lately, I don't see many people really really drinking at parties. Not like in the heyday of Studio 54 when I actually saw someone being carried *into* a party. Not out of it—Into It! I don't drink very much now myself, but I like to go to a party with an open bar because then you know that more people will be in a good mood and that it isn't a cheapo party because at least they're splurging.

I would love to be a good toaster—stand up there, go bang-bang on the glass, and give people a lump in their throats. "Well put! Shakespeare couldn't have said it better!" Toasting is like delivering a eulogy—people hang on every word. I watched magazine editor Danny Fields at the wedding of our mutual friend Susan Blond to Roger Erickson. Danny was the best man and he knew he'd have to toast the couple—he'd looked it up in every etiquette book and realized there was no way out. He was terrified. One book said do it with the cake, one said without the cake, one said do it before they sit down, one said *after*. . . . He had set aside a whole weekend to think about it, and in the end he did get something lovely out of his mouth, but I could see that until it was over, he was a nervous wreck; his whole day was anxiety. It spoils a dinner for you if you feel toast vibrations coming your way—that somebody is actually going to ask you to do it. You don't relax until you finally hear that scraping sound as the first chair pulls back and you know the dinner's over and you're safe.

It's a rare talent, toasting well, and when somebody's good, you really notice it. Usually, though, toasts are just embarrassing and we could do without them, unless some born-to-toast personality like, say, Gore Vidal happens to be at the table with something on his mind that he's bursting to say.

Thank-you notes. Go by your instincts on whether to send them or not. You sort of have an intuition, usually, of what's going to be mean-ingful to people, and then you know whether to bother writing it or just saying it to them. It's easy enough to write something like, "Once again, your hospitality was out of this world, and I'm looking forward to seeing you again real soon." If it's someone like somebody's mother, this will mean a lot to her. On the other hand, video director Don Munroe had the casual urban party-goer's attitude when he told me, "I never write thank-you notes, no. But I do call the next day to make sure everybody's okay—I make concerned phone calls."

Boy George and Quentin Crisp

Clubs

When the Palladium opened down on 14th Street back in 1985, it redefined the discotheque "party," because in a place that huge (it was once a movie palace, the Academy of Music), they could throw multiple parties every night—sometimes all in the same room. In the private area they called the Michael Todd Room, they sometimes had as many as three parties going at the same time, so that if you happened to step backwards just so you wouldn't get burned by a cigarette, you found yourself in another party! Over here was the party for the fashion designer, over there was the party for the new magazine, over there was the rock-and-roll party. . . . You'd walk through the room going, "What party is this?" And, "Which party is that over in the corner?" "What party am I in now?"

Around that time the major clubs all started having enormous mailing lists and they began sending out thousands of free and thousands more of "You're-invited-but-you-have-to-pay" invitations every week. When he booked events at the Palladium, party impresario Rudolf kept on the wall of his office a list of the lists they used for mailings—numbers with notations next to them that characterized the type of crowd on that particular list. Things like, "Downtown, but not necessarily gay," "Rich and boring," "Fashion victims," "Fashion perpetrators," etc. When you managed to figure out which list/lists you were on, it was like getting to read your F.B.I. file—you knew what they thought about you, how you'd been categorized. You'd wind up getting multiple invitations to the same party when you were on more than one list. I always wondered what compulsive Joan Crawford—who stretched etiquette to the point where she sent thank-you cards for Christmas cards—would do if she were alive to get "disco mail." She'd be busy for the rest of her life: "Thanks for the five invitations to your charming party for the Male Model of the Year". . . .

The Palladium was created in May 1985 by Steve Rubell and Ian Schrager, and it went strong through most of 1986 until it started to die out that fall. To get a picture of how fast and how big the "discotheque party" grew, just compare the Palladium with Steve and Ian's first New York City club, the legendary Studio 54. When Studio opened in the mid-Seventies, it revived nightlife in the city, which had gone semi-dormant at the end of the Sixties. Since the Palladium would sometimes have four or five parties in one *night*, it's amazing to remember that in the early days of Studio, there were only four big parties a *year*, really—New Year's, Valentine's, Halloween, and always a refurbishing party when it reopened each September with a new look. Sure, they wanted to pack people in, but they relied on word of mouth, really, and, except for the big, big parties, they didn't do the heavy-volume invitation-mailing that became par in the mid-Eighties. People would usually just show up or they'd hear about the party over the phone, because the whole network that 54 started—the New York nightlife—was spontaneous. And then there were a few additional theme parties and celebrity parties, but no more than probably one a month. And each one was spectacular. They did one for Elizabeth Taylor where they had thousands of gardenias—her favorite—and they even somehow got the Rockettes from Radio City to come over and do a birthday kick for her, holding three-foot sparklers. At Studio 54, you got very special treatment and Steve himself was always running around and personally making sure everything was fabulous. He and Ian would go all out and spare no extravagance.

I remember a country-western party they did for Dolly Parton where Renny Reynolds, the party designer who did the staging there for the first three years, created a whole barnyard scene for Dolly with live animals and hay and spotlights on big shucked cornstalks growing in huge tubs. It was August and Renny had trucked everything up from his farm in Pennsylvania. The next morning, he told me, he found one of his poor goats still in the balcony, "probably drugged up but good"—but they

34

Steve Rubell thriving on rejection: "No, you're not on the list—you'd bring your tacky electrician friends!"

all did make it back to the farm in one piece, and Dolly loved them. And then I remember one New Year's Eve they built eight walls of ice and covered the floor with stainless steel in the entrance hall, and then the rest of the place was all Styrofoam packing. The blocks of ice were so big they didn't melt; they had pumps built underneath.

At Studio 54, every big party was so thought-out and designed, it was as if they were building a city. They reinforced the theme in every nook and cranny. It was so "done" and so much went into them. But at the Palladium, it was just too big for anyone to care as much about detail. Palladium was a volume place—like walking into Macy's, lots of different departments. And like Macy's, it had to do a certain volume every day or night.

Most clubs in Manhattan make their money selling drinks, not on admission. When they have "champagne parties" they don't make money on that by itself, but it does bring people in, and lots of them are sure to stay on and buy drinks after the free champagne ends, or they'll tell their friends to meet them there and those friends will buy drinks. So that explains why a club will throw a party for somebody for no great reason—"So-and-so Invites You to Celebrate So-and-so's Safe Arrival off the Long Island Expressway from a Weekend in East Hampton." Or in honor of somebody's getting his green card—momentous things like that. I got invited to a party that I thought someone was giving for his *sweater,* although it turned out to be just a Sweater Party—just one where everybody was supposed to *wear* a sweater. The thing was, at that particular point, somebody giving a party for something as ridiculous as his sweater wasn't impossible. In fact, I actually had made plans to go, to see what this sweater being honored could possibly look like. If something else hadn't come up, I would have gone.

By mid-1986 when the party-every-night club scene peaked, it had gotten so huge, it was literally *thousands* of great-looking kids. I was always shocked when I looked around Area or the World or the Limelight or the Tunnel that I didn't know every single one of them, because in the Sixties, if there was somebody with a "look," you al-ways knew them. Danny Fields explained it this way: "It became a new party world. In the Sixties, one lone man—Mickey Ruskin at the door of Max's Kansas City—could control the quality of the crowd that came in. Today, all you have to do to be considered interesting is dress up, and that option is available to hundreds of thousands of people. And they look as good as real people, so you don't know until you stop and ask them a few questions that all they did *was* dress up—that all they are are nobodies dressed up. The old party world was that you were always somebody whether you were dressed up or not, and you were always fabulous because you were who you were."

What Danny pointed out about Mickey Ruskin, the *owner* of Max's, also acting as its hands-on *doorman* back in the Sixties, underscores how quaint the scene was then compared to today. Who could imagine Nell Campbell herself standing out on West 14th Street, hand-picking her club's clientele every night? More on Nell's and its doormen later.

Jeffrey Slonim and Ginger McFadden

Paige Powell

Writer Fran Lebowitz, radio producer Danny Fields, Susan Blond, and Roger Erickson on opening night of the Palladium

Tere Tereba using the Kenny Scharf phones in the basement of the Palladium.

Michael Musto, Madelaine Netter, and the mosaic toilet, a temporary fixture at Area's front door

DAVID JOHANSEN

Since David Johansen's days as a New York Doll, he's had a new incarnation as "Buster Poindexter," and as I was leaving a party at the Palladium one night, I ran into music critic Glenn O'Brien, who was on his way to see him perform at Tramps, just around the corner on 15th Street. I tagged along and saw David's act. He performs elegantly, in a tuxedo, and between shows we talked about the kinds of private events he plays at.

What kind of music do you perform?

We're getting into a gray area here. Let's just call it Americana.

When you're not working the clubs in New York, where do you play?

At a lot of parties. We play lots of resorts, so we do power bar mitzvahs and things like that.

Do you ever play balls?

Small balls. I have been called the Peter Duchin of the punk set.

Do you get paid well?

Plenty.

How much is plenty?

Try to imagine what "plenty" would mean to a man like me.

Do you go to many club parties? I mean, as a guest?

No. At this point, when I go to a club, it's like a busman's holiday. Which means, of course, doing on your day off what you do for a living. Like if Ralph Kramden took Alice for a drive in the country? I play so much in clubs, that going to a club for a party isn't a thrill. I mean, when I'm finished here I'm not going to race over to the Palladium for one of those parties to "honor" a male model. You know?

What about festivals? Did either one of you go to Woodstock?

Glenn did, I believe. *(Glenn nods yes.)* I went to Altamont. And I had a wonderful time, incidentally—I had no idea anyone was getting killed. Where *I* was, it was fabulous.

David's last point illustrates a broad party principle: The fun you have at a party can depend on WHAT PART OF THE PARTY you're in. You can be in a good part of a bad party, like he was at Altamont, or you can be in a bad part of a good party, like stuck at a bad table at a great dinner.

> The night the Palladium opened, it felt like you were in Saigon during the last days with the helicopters coming down and everyone hysterical to get on. People were diving under the ropes, it was so dramatic. When I was going in, everyone dived underneath me and the bouncers ran over to help Haoui and Sally—the doormen— and in my mind it seems like the bouncers had machine guns. Of course they didn't, but it was like that kind of feeling. Suddenly I was pushed back into the club and they pulled down those heavy metal gates like garage doors—and people were diving under them as they came down, rolling around on the concrete floor in their tuxedos and evening gowns, desperate to get in.
> Madelaine Netter

RUDOLF

Club owner and manager Rudolf is an idea person—a clubmeister who loves the nightlife and sees it as an art form. He's businesslike and professional; you never even see him drinking when he walks through the parties—it's as if he's checking the stock in a store, seeing if he's got enough shoes out on the rack. And yet he drives a car that Tony Montana would be thrilled with, and every night when he leaves his own club (or clubs, if he's involved with more than one at that moment) he goes on to every other club in the city. He shows up in any obscure places, looking to spot trends that are coming up. In eighty-six he took a break from running his own clubs to work for the Palladium, where his job was to make sure that the huge place was completely booked with parties every night. Working on that big a commercial scale, and coordinating a volume of party traffic that heavy, he couldn't indulge in the idea snobbery that he can when he does his smaller, fun clubs, but still, somehow, he always made sure that nothing sank below a certain level. He came to New York in the late seventies from Germany via Brazil, and he recommends that all Germans spend some time in Rio or São Paulo just "to take the edges off." I talked to him one afternoon in the office he had then at the Palladium.

To think up parties and make them happen on a big, professional scale, what's the most important quality a person needs?

Being quite cold about it. You need to examine everybody and everything for its Party Value. It's subjective. You rate something on how it looks, how commercial it is, how much fun—one glance and you get it. It's calculating, but not completely. Because maybe a person has no Party Value, but I could still do many other things with this person, like, say, get laid.

That's like that line in *Saturday Night Fever* when the John Travolta character says, "Just because you fuck a girl doesn't mean you have to dance with her."

Right. Everybody has his function. It's like being a stock-exchange operator. Which I once was. You're examining shares and instantly you take into account all the factors, from the glamour of the moment to the whole health of the corporation, and in one second you know, "Okay, I want to buy it." With parties, it's visual: Does it attract the eye? Here at Palladium I coordinate all the activities of the club. We have two/three/four parties a day here, sometimes as many as five. Usually seven days a week. I get paid a salary and not a commission because I don't want to have a vested interest in any party. Temptation is there when a huge party will bring in five thousand—but it would only be good for the pocketbook, not for the career. This is as big as I can go in clubland (*laughs*), unless somebody has the balls to make a bigger place than this.

Since parties are your business,

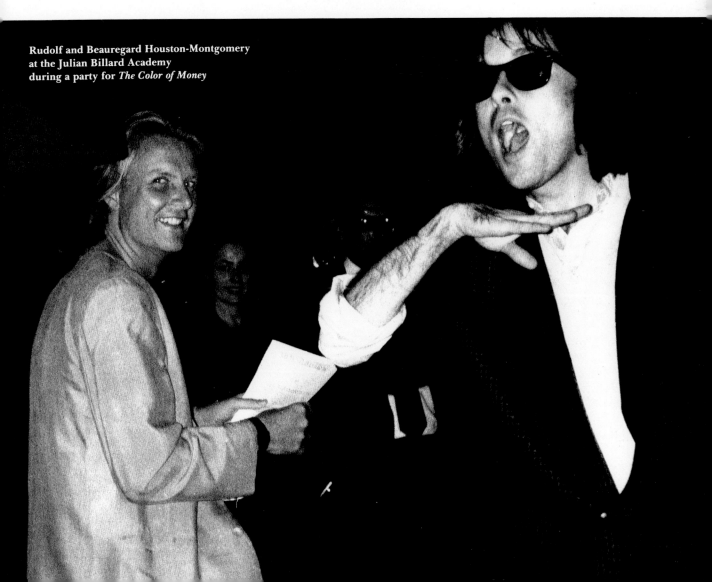

Rudolf and Beauregard Houston-Montgomery at the Julian Billard Academy during a party for *The Color of Money*

where do you go for pleasure?

Every night about midnight I leave here and I go out to every other club. It takes me three or four hours. I enjoy it. I go wherever a personal appearance seems called for. Or I could just go to Harlem, you know, to Small's Paradise, because maybe there's a good band playing there that I might want to book for here. Bronx, Queens, I go everywhere. I have a car. During the day a car is useless in New York, but at night you can park in front of any place you're going, easily. There's a whole section of Queens that's wild. Roosevelt Avenue with the Colombians. Real intense people. You'll always end up in the house of some guy and there's tons of coke and guns. I speak Spanish. If I didn't, they'd think I was CIA. I lived in South America for eight years. I did the first "pub" in Brazil. It was just a bar, but if it has a name that's European or American, they love it. My friend Ronald Biggs had a club in Rio and mine was in São Paulo. My first club was in Germany, in Berlin, in sixty-eight. I came here in seventy-nine, and Brazil was in between. Things are not so hard-edged in South America. It's a valuable education. Among themselves, Latins will always cut a deal. "Okay, we're going to make an apprehension now. Give us half the coke and half the money and we'll, you know, split. . . ."

Where do you look for inspiration to get a theme for a party?

I like people, so I go everywhere to see what they're talking about. I might go down to the Pyramid to see what the hell they're doing there. If they're presenting an idea, it's always raw, so if it's interesting, I'll take that raw idea—that candy—put chocolate around it, wrap it up in bright shiny paper, and then it's a party for Palladium that makes sense for this place. In America there's no magazine worth reading; show business is self-explanatory. I read certain foreign magazines for ideas. Or I get two different ideas and put them together. That's what "Dime a Dance" was a few weeks ago. I was having the Chiffons sing at two-thirty in

Peter Gaitien, owner of the Limelight

the morning, and that was something to do on a winter night, but still I knew it needed more. So I add Anita DJ—Anita Sarko. But still it needed something. I happened to be reading a magazine from the forties and I saw those ten-cent girls in Times Square, and that's how I put that together. A big success—everybody loved it. People are very demanding, but on the other hand, they really like simple things. Simple but clever. Themes have gotten ultrasophisticated in the last few years. In the early days of Studio 54 they would give parties with themes like "A Salute to Springtime," and it actually brought everybody out!

Lots of times people get more than one invitation to the same party. Why does that happen?

The invitations go out by computer. We have exactly one hundred mailing lists here right now. They were collected painfully over the years. Forty-seven of them are mine that I collected during the five years of Danceteria. When I work with these different small lists, I can find two or three that will make each specific party work. For instance, let's say I have a downtown artist, but he's selling a lot uptown and we're having a cocktail party for him. I'll pick one of the downtown small-club lists, and then use the Leo Castelli list for the uptown buyers crowd, and then I'll want some fun so I'll use maybe the *Details* magazine list, and then maybe an art-press list, and there I'd have a list-cocktail that works. One particular person may be on more than one of the lists I choose, and that's why some people get more than one invitation sometimes.

What kinds of parties do you turn down here at the Palladium?

Those that're crassly commercial, just some company plugging a product. If the company wants, we'll let them do it in the afternoon or on Monday night when the club is rented out, and they have to pay dearly for it.

Lately, you haven't had food much at parties. Like in the Mike Todd Room, it's usually just drinks.

I tend to stay away from food because I see it as nonessential and messy. It smells, it gives people bad breath, and I have to take all this into account. I'm a professional and I don't want this kind of thing to happen. It's *unbelievably* messy—it gets on chairs and you sit in it. And then there's the lighting problem: When food is lit, the whole lighting scheme of the floor gets unbalanced. Especially if the food is taken away at a certain point. Because you can't turn off the light unless you get a guy on a ladder. See, it's all theatrical lighting in a club like this, so it's plugs. And of course it can't be a green or blue or red light—it has to be white or pink. Also, the food looks great on the menu that the caterer gives you, but when it arrives it's not what you thought it was. And however much it is, it's never enough. Never, never enough, no matter how much you spend. You see, these are problems that somebody with three drinks will never notice, but a professional will.

Don't you feel sorry for the people outside who never get in? The Palladium is so big, it's like not getting into Madison Square Garden; it's pathetic.

Sure it's heartbreaking, but this is New York! People have access to every piece of information in the world—therefore, if they don't get the message of how to behave and dress and *be*, then they're dumb idiots and deserve to eat shit. What's their excuse in New York City for not knowing how to dress? Sure, Palladium is big, but you don't want it filled with creeps.

Do you keep scrapbooks of your parties?

Only if I think there might be some liability, if I have an intuition that some journalist or lawyer will come up with something.

Do you do a contract for every party?

Not every one. *(laughs)* I *know* the parties I should make a contract for. But many times when it's a simple party you don't write a contract at all, unless the person wants one.

Anita Sarko

Escaping the crush of opening night at the Limelight in Chicago. Chris Makos in fishnet

If anything goes wrong at a party, I hang on to all the records. I keep them for a year or two, but people can still sue you three years later, sometimes! But other than for legal reasons, I don't keep records. No scrapbooks. The beauty of the nightlife is that it just lasts the moment and then it's gone. No boring archives is ever going to have it.

Do you get sued a lot?

Danceteria got sued from forty to sixty times a year. I haven't lost a case, but I went through a judicial agreement twice. Most of the cases at Danceteria, because of its layout, were people falling down the stairs. But a lot of cases went to the Human Rights Commission. If they're refused, they say it's religion or race or sex. For instance, I didn't want groups of men at Danceteria—they had to come with ladies. So that's "sexual discrimination."

I love what Rudolf pointed out about the lawsuits from people who didn't get into the club winding up at the Human Rights Commission. All over the world there are human-rights organizations fighting to get people out of gulags and torture chambers—only in America would the Human Rights Commission be working to get people *into* parties.

DIANNE BRILL

Dianne Brill is a fashion designer who makes nobodies feel like somebodies with the big hellos she gives to everybody. She was the first young girl in decades to really play up a big body with big curves and big cleavage. In mid-eighty-six, when the following conversation took place, she operated full tilt all night all over New York as the ultimate Party Girl and earned herself the title "Queen of the Night."

Just tell me about parties, Dianne.

I go anywhere for a party, uptown or downtown. I integrate anywhere. I started going out just for fun. Little did I know it was going to turn into such an organized discipline. Let's say there are three

Dianne Brill and Michael Gross

things to do in a night. Instead of doing what I used to do, which was to do all three, I pick the best party, I go for an hour, and then I split. If I'm on a roll, I try to hit the *peaks* of the parties. You know a party's peaking when there stops being an influx of people in and out. You feel a stagnant point: Everybody's there, everybody's having fun and talking, but there aren't new people coming in; it's the same people in the same area and the energy is just about to go down. And *that's* when you arrive—"I'M HERE!" You're the new one, you're dressed, and hopefully you get a positive reaction. After you get that reaction, the energy level starts to drop and you get the hell out of there. It's like physics—the energy, the light, the sound, the visual impact, the exchange.

The more parties you go to, the sharper your intuition gets. I'll sense when "this" party will be better than "that" one, and I'm usually right. You look at who's involved, where it is, what time of day it is, what time of year it is for the circumstance, and so on. Let's say there's one party at a small club, another at a big club, and another at a restaurant in, say, Tribeca. You ask people all day where they're going, and you see which types of people are going where. Maybe you'll notice that all the secretaries and runners in people's offices are going to the one at the small club, and you'll know that that party is going to have too much volume to be any good. So you decide to hit it early, because later it's going to be too crowded. In a case like that you don't aim for the peak because it's irrelevant—you just want to go before it's overrun. You sacrifice the peak for hip.

It's good to have integration, but you don't want to have people who go, "Wow, is that your real hair? Are you from New York?" Retardos. If you suspect it's going to be like that, go during the first half hour and then leave, because that's when all the interesting people will be there, since they know what you know—that it's not going to be a long-run fun party. They may even skip it altogether, and you may, too.

I do my own clothes. I don't actually sew, but I design everything I wear. My visuals are crucial. Not everybody has to have a party dress on, but if I'm hosting a party, I have to wear something completely out of the usual. It has to be in the *mode* of what I usually do, but stepped up a few speeds. Sometimes when I'm in a quiet mood, I'll tone it down; I'll just wear a skintight latex turtleneck, as opposed to a low-cut bustier something. I mean, it's always *fitted,* but sometimes instead of showing cleavage I'll just feel like a high-neck wool jersey.

I like men in suits, but not office-type suits. White-knight clothes. Hero clothes. Nino Cerutti would be the ideal escort.

I was brought up in Wisconsin and Florida. In Florida we had a big house and a pool and cabanas, and my parents would give luaus. People would come in Hawaiian garb. I have very charismatic parents, so I was raised with the party mentality. I learned integration from them—getting the cream of every crop. It's like the "new money" mentality; you mix people up. I would sit on my mother's bed and watch her stroke on her makeup, and watch my dad do up the buttons of his tuxedo, and then wait for them to come home and bring me party favors or hors d'oeuvres. They included me in their evening even when I wasn't there. My father knew how to host. He'd walk into a room crowded with people and invite them all to dinner at a restaurant. I remember the feeling of power he put out—he was a social magician.

Certain foods at parties are a mistake. When Mexican food was around, everyone would have beans and guacamole on their breath. It's not a social food! Sushi is a social food, but sushi's dated. Chocolate is a social food.

I like sit-down dinners. A lot of people don't because it's slow. But you can get deeper with people you've never really talked to. We did a fantastic sit-down for about two hundred people once at Danceteria. Rudolf and I do great parties together, because I'm good at the hostessing and making it happen, and he's great at organizing it. It was my birthday, but just to do a birthday isn't enough. So at the time those "Coffee Achievers" commercials were running on TV, and they were so absurd. One had the two girls from Heart in a studio talking about how coffee kept them awake and helped them do their best, and then it said, "Coffee calms you down: It gives you the serenity to dream and the vitality to do it." And in another one they had a football segment and they're drinking the coffee and planning the game strategy and then they throw the chair across the room and go play ball. Like, everything was violent. The commercials were all so absurd that I fell in love with them, and they would come up in my conversation all day. I happen to be a big coffee drinker. So that became the theme for my birthday: the Coffee Achievers.

That was one of the best parties I've ever been to.

Wasn't it fun? We did a beautiful décor with enormous coffee beans, and it was a total environment, things happening all the time—talking on the phone drinking coffee, vignettes, push-up bras and stuff. I had a guy do all the costuming and Rudolf booked the band and put it all together. We had the Shirelles come out and sing Happy Birthday to me, and while we were eating, tons of acts came out, all girls dressed like me—clones—doing coffee poses.

Did a girl as popular as you ever have to pay to get into clubs?

Sure. When I first came to town. It didn't last long, but I did pay at first.

What's your philosophy?

I've always been a cheerleader type, just getting things rolling and making them go—"Let's have fun!" And then you do. There's a lot of affection going on. It feeds me, going out. You have to *give.* But you also get a lot. After I've gone out, it's hard to fall asleep right away, even though I'm exhausted. I don't drink or do drugs. Since I come from Florida, naturally I did at one time, but I got tired of it pretty quickly. It didn't wear well on me. I could never do what I do if I even

Celebrating Harley-Davidson night at Area. Matt Dillon observes from the mezzanine

had one drink, because it's so much work and discipline and persistence—the rhythm is important, and drugs just unfocus me.

What's the biggest party you ever had?

Six thousand people were at my birthday party at the Palladium in 1985—I wanted a mega-party. My actual birthday is in early April, but the Palladium hadn't opened yet, so finally on June twenty-ninth the time was right. I got a lot of Cancer cards.

Do you do your own invitations?

I have combination lists. Fashion, music, art, social, downtown trendies and uptown ones, plus all my business lists, which I do include sometimes, depending on the party, how big it is. I take my lists and look at them and do a spot-check edit, because people move or maybe they're not going out anymore, or there are a lot of new people you're missing. When you're having a mega-party, you take over the whole club, but then you take the hip room of the club and make it for the elite, say, five hundred. Then you do maybe five thousand other invitations.

How do you get so much press?

I certainly don't have press agents. I mean, if you wrote a column and I hounded you, would you be in a hurry to put me in? Today I'm devoting a lot of time to designing clothes, so I have to be realistic—I go out for half an hour, an hour, and then I split. I never made any money going to parties or doing them, but I had a lot of fun. Now I'm trying to incorporate parties into my life, instead of having them *be* my life.

ANN MAGNUSON

From March 1979 to September 1980, writer-actress Ann Magnuson ran Club 57 on St. Marks Place, where they did a lot of theme parties. (Kenny Scharf and Keith Haring had some of their early art shows there.) She also organized events at the Mudd Club and the Underground—and things like an Italian Night at Danceteria, where they strung laundry across the alley, and the

Festival of San De Niro, where they had a big picture of Bobby De Niro from his movie True Confessions *and people would pay to tape paper money onto it (they served pasta and had a puppet show that was scenes from Francis Ford Coppola movies done by puppets Punch 'n' Judy style.)*

Where did you come from?

West Virginia. Charleston. I went to school in Ohio and London and came here on a work-study program in 1978. I wanted to direct plays. But I was drawn to downtown. I'd read your book *Popism* and I thought, Oooh, I want to know all about those things, and I got more sucked into what was going on down there, more interested in the "avant garde" than in Neil Simon. I directed a show at Irving Plaza called "New Wave Vaudeville," and the people there also had Club 57, so that's how I started there. It was under a Polish church. Sean and Eric from Area used to come a lot. When I was doing things there, the Mudd Club was sort of doing things too, but we tended to be more obscure. These friends of mine—Tom Scully and Susan Hannaford-Rose—wanted to have a Monster Movie Club every Tuesday, so they set that up, and I had the rest of the nights and started making up theme parties. This was in 1979.

What were some of the themes?

We had "The Model World of Glue," and it was like a glue-sniffing party where you built Aurora models. We put a bag with glue on each table and people really got into building their models and burning them and pouring glue on the flames. And we had the "Wild Wild World of Speed," which wasn't speedy because the person who was supposed to get the speed didn't bring it. It was kind of a bust.

But that's actually what a typical speed party was like—waiting for the speed to arrive.

In that case, it was a kind of success. And we had one called "Twistin' in High Society," and everyone had to come in Sixties-style formal wear, and I turned the

TV personality Mary Hart

Tina Turner

floor into a Twister Board by making giant color spots with contact paper. It was like creating your own movie. So if you had "James Bond Night," people would dress as Bond characters and create their own play, and we'd do the soundtrack and the décor. My perception was that it was a time machine, so you'd have, say, "Psychedelic Night," and everyone would come as hippies and you could actually do acid and mescaline. We had "Beatnik Night" and "Country Music Night"—we put hay all over the floor—and "Voodoo Night," which was wild. It was like therapy. In fact, we *had* "Therapy Night."

How would people find out what was happening?

I made up calendars and newsletters and we had a membership and gave out cards. The membership was only about one hundred twenty people; it was very much a neighborhood thing. Lots of the concepts for parties that the big clubs have had in the last few years have been variations on things that we did. Like we'd done a six-hole miniature golf course in the club and made it look like a Jamaican shantytown and called it "Putt Putt Reggae" and played reggae and ska music and only ten people showed up. Palladium did a miniature-golf-course thing and they even admitted to me, "Well, we know you did it at Club 57, but, gee, that was so long ago."

Did you ever have any problems with lawsuits?

No, because we were totally illegal. And we obviously had no money, so who could be bothered to sue us? We were underneath a church, we had a bar, the whole thing was ridiculous. It closed and now it's a mental-health outpatient clinic.

You're acting in feature films now, but do you ever went to go back to staging events?

Yes. I want to do my own Broadway show, and I want a TV show so I can apply my ideas to that area. Although when I'm older I could see myself having my own club again, kind of like Miss Kitty on *Gunsmoke*.

NICK BEAVERS, TOBY BEAVERS, AND JOHN MULLER

The three Beavers brothers, Toby, Angus, and Nick, were born and raised on upper Fifth Avenue, descended from Beekmans and Devereauxs. The family has a steel foundry, but the boys hit it big on their own when they opened the Surf Club and later the Zulu Lounge, both on the Upper East Side. Preppy/yuppie clubs with "That Touch of Beaver." Their mother, Pat, financed them, and John Muller, an ex-model, is a partner. I went up to the Surf Club one night and talked to Nick and Toby and John.

What's your door policy?

NB: It's basically a yuppie crowd, so anyone who has a gray suit on gets in. We'll let the Wild Bunch in every so often if they look like fun, but those usually go down to Zulu.

I only go to clubs for half an hour.

NB: Well, fine. If I operated that way, I'd go to the big clubs once a month to see their new thing, their new art installations or whatever. But if you want to go where there's people you know, who you can at least sit down and talk with, then you establish a crew place. It's like a local pub in England. No matter where they start off at night, they'll end up here. Sometimes they'll start off *and* end up here, but they'll always end here. You can start at eleven o'clock and go to a downtown club for a dip, and then if you come back here and still strike out, there's always the after-hours bars that open at four or six A.M. If you haven't gotten loaded enough to sleep, or if you haven't gotten what you wanted, there's a lot of illegal gambling places. These go right into the afternoon.

Yes, but if you haven't gotten whatever it is you want to get by four in the morning, it's better to go home, it really is. Because at these after-hours clubs, they frisk you and lock the door behind you, and suddenly you're in there with some real criminals. Not just the petty criminals like you get at the regular clubs, but major, major felons. Why did you start the Surf Club?

Amanda Plummer and Andrew McCarthy

Matthew Rolston

Matt Dillon and Paige Powell

NB: There were no Upper East Side rock bars—no music places uptown except for JP's, which was an old sort of place on Seventy-sixth and First. James Taylor and Carly Simon used to play there. We wanted to get something going on a weird night like Sunday. Very few people uptown went out on Sunday night. Downtown they did.

TB: All we ever wanted to do was get laid. Now we don't even have to make phone calls anymore—they all flock here. They get real drunk and then we have our pick. It's dark in the club, but we can take them to the offices on the side so we can check them in the bright lights for zits or boils. The first year I gave away so much liquor because I didn't know what I was doing. That's what goes on every night. Like this birthday party we're in the middle of now. It's a friend, and her sister's having a birthday so I said, "Give 'em a case." I'll go around in a couple of hours and see what I can scare up. It's like a badger coming out of his hole: I *know* there's somebody out there that needs it. Although it could end up in my hand.

NB: Your hand needs it.

TB: It happens to everybody.

NB: No, if you have a girlfriend, you can just go home early.

TB: But then you're so bored that you're making believe she's somebody else, anyway. I made it with "ten different girls" the other night. And then I lost it. Ha ha ha.

NB: I don't know, I still have to get moderately buzzed to take any forward action.

TB: Of course! I mean, can you imagine making it with anybody *sober?* The breath odors coming up, surrounding your nostrils? . . . I just got a prescription for Antabuse. I'm seeing this big doctor for coke and drugs. He wants me to go on it tonight for two weeks to see if I can enjoy my life without being fucked-up drunk. I'm very happy with my life, but I just want to go into fantasies sometimes and be trashed. And I think it's much more fun, plus I get to forget everything I've done. Therefore every day when I wake up it's something new. If I ever remembered *(laughs),* I'd never come back here.

Club owner Nick Beavers with a friend in his office at the Surf Club

NB: That's right. It's no fun talking three sentences to forty different people. The *same* three sentences: "Hi. How are you? Can I get you a drink?" I mean, if you sit around *any* club and listen to the small talk, you just fucking fall asleep. You'd just tell them, "Shit. You are so boring." But after five drinks, you're buzzed and anything is hysterical—somebody tells you, "I played golf yesterday," and it's hilarious.

TB: John here hasn't had a drink in—how many years is it, John?

JM: I started again last week. I started again basically because I was getting sick of drugs. It's better to alternate a little. I've never stopped both. I don't think I've been completely straight for a day in the last twenty years.

NB: To be honest, I can say that I haven't been completely straight for two consecutive days since I was seventeen. I started really young going to all the punk clubs. The first place I went to was CBGBs. If you could get your head over the bar, they'd let you in. In boarding school I remember at least three days a week getting trashed. I can't smoke pot. I'm twenty-one now and I started so early that I'm sick of hallucinogenics. I'm burning out on cocaine—every so often I'll do it and get wired and hate it and then someone'll offer it to me again when I'm loaded and I'll go through the whole thing again. . . .

There's so much legal red tape involved in running clubs in the city—permits and things. Do you have problems with inspectors who want to be bribed and things like that?

NB: When we first opened, we didn't know how you did it, so we never got started—we were so naïve, they didn't know how to tell us they wanted to be bribed. Instead of sending higher and higher people to deal with them, we'd send lower and lower. We'd have the busboy who doesn't talk English go and deal with them.

JM: We did everything legally and still they kept coming on and on, so I just got fed up. We'd build walls they said we needed and then they'd come back and say, "Gee, I still see lot of violations." So finally I just said, "Gee, well, then start writing them up." Because otherwise, if you bribe them, it never ends.

What are your long-range plans?

TB: We're liquidating a small steel company that our father left us in Pennsylvania. We can't make any money that way anymore with all the imports—Korea, Brazil, Taiwan, Yugoslavia. . . .

Did you get your club personalities from your father?

TB: He's dead now. We're Dutch. My father thought he was a playboy, and he ran around snaking kind of unattractive girls, and he was pretty pompous—

NB: I'd speak better of him than that.

TB: But the girls—I mean, remember the one with legs like gas tanks and a thirty-six-inch waist?

NB: Well, come on! The guy was forty years old! He was looking for a relationship, not a piece of ass! At least for a while he was, and then I guess he just gave up. You know, "Fuck it, I'll stick with ass."

TB: Oh, but he'd always have some comment to make about *our* girls, though: "She's cute, but she's got a fat ass." I'd say, "Well, look at the ass on *yours!* Talk about fat!" And he'd say, "Sure, but mine have personality—yours are stupid." And to our mother all our girls were sluts because we'd yank them into our rooms after school.

NB: My mother had this thing where I was not allowed to get caught in bed with a girl unless I'd known her two weeks or something like that. My room was on the second floor, so I'd sneak out the window and take the bus down to Xenon or someplace, and with a little luck I'd bum taxi fare home and by that time my mother would be totally asleep.

What kind of girls do you like? What's your type?

TB: *Anything's* my type (*turning to the girl next to him*). A couple of drinks and *you'll* be my type.

As I left the Surf Club I heard a couple of girls talking. One said, "You forget what dating was like in

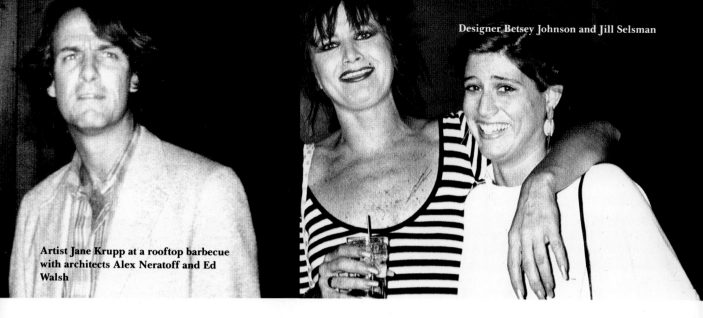

Designer Betsey Johnson and Jill Selsman

Artist Jane Krupp at a rooftop barbecue with architects Alex Neratoff and Ed Walsh

college, but when you meet the Beavers, they bring it all back." And her girlfriend said, "Yeah, in *triplicate*."

At a certain point in the Seventies, giving parties at home began to seem kind of corny. The punk, destructive attitude was the style and giving a party isn't a negative thing—it's sort of a cute, positive thing to do. People seemed to prefer going out to see the B-52s or the Talking Heads in a club to sitting around somebody's apartment talking, and anyway, it just got too wild to give big parties at home in Manhattan with the security problems. Instead, places like the Mudd Club began giving theme parties. It had always seemed odd and abstract to me, anyway, to have a party in your own home, right where you *live*—letting people, some of them strangers, wander through your private life. I feel that if you can't hide what you are where you *live*, where are you supposed to hide it? I only give parties away from my house. But even people who had always thrown big bashes at home began to do anything larger than dinner parties in clubs and restaurants—at home they just didn't have the size of apartment or the security force that you need to have a party, with the amount of people who were showing up every place for everything from sheer force of party-going habit. And in fact, the kids who got used to going to clubs all the time for parties started to go

nuts when they found themselves at a "house party." John Sex told me, "I get claustrophobia in someone's house, because in a nightclub you can leave at any point, but at somebody's house, you feel really weird getting up and leaving, like you're being rude and saying it's the end of the party. In L.A. you do go to big parties at people's houses, but not in New York." And then I asked photographer Christopher Makos when was the last party he went to at someone's house, and he looked blank for a minute and then said, "Gee, I don't know—it must have been out of state."

THE PHANTOM BALL

Architect Alexandr Neratoff and artist Jane Krupp gave three big New Year's Eve parties in Alex's Soho loft, and their experiences during the third (and final) one show some of the problems of "entertaining at home" and why most people began to have parties at clubs, rather than in their own homes (even when they live in spaces as big as Alex's). His two-thousand-square-foot loft is a white-columned, scarlet-walled "ballroom" with wainscoting and chestnut molding. The building dates back to 1879, and since his place on the second floor used to be a pharmaceutical company, it has terracotta floors that made it fireproof. Alex is active in the Russian emigré community, organizing charity events and things, and the loft has an Imperial Russian feeling—it's magical at night, with long white curtains blowing and big candles flickering. He and

Jane gave their first Scarlet Ball there on New Year's Eve in 1981.

JK: There was a rumor going around that somebody committed suicide at our third annual Scarlet Ball, but what happened was this girl who we'd never seen before runs screaming out of the bathroom, "She cut her wrist!" By then it was three-thirty A.M. on New Year's Eve and the boiler had broken down about midnight so I was shivering in my ballgown with bare shoulders.

AN: I look in the bathroom and see that the sink has collapsed onto the floor and there's just a ceramic shard sticking up from the pedestal. Three people were in there, still, so I presume they'd been sitting on the sink taking drugs and it just came out of the wall. There was blood everywhere, it looked like *Psycho*—on the floor, the walls—and one girl held up her hand and it was almost severed at the wrist. She didn't seem to be in pain or anything—she wasn't even whimpering.

JK: Remember, we have never seen these people before. The people who arrive at three o'clock on New Year's are so drunk already that they're coming to your place basically to throw up and use your bathroom. And they're desperate for something to eat, so no matter what's left out, it goes—cream cheese smeared on the platters, anything. I've found them in the kitchen looking for cooking sherry.

AN: I made an announcement that the party was over and the people this girl had come with put a tourniquet on her bicep. Then I called an ambulance, but fifteen minutes later they called back and said, "Unfortunately we're very busy—it's New Year's Eve and we don't have one to send."

JK: So the lesson there is that not only can't you get a cab on New Year's Eve—you can't even get an ambulance!

AN: Her friends got her with her arm up so the blood would stay in, and she's still not complaining so I have to assume she was heavily narcotized. I told her friends that the ambulance wouldn't come and they said, "Then we'll take her." They had a car, it turned out, so I don't know why they didn't take her in the first place. Then they started fighting over which hospital to take her to. Shostakovich's grandson was there, Dimitri, and his father came to pick him up, only he arrived just as they were carrying this girl out of the elevator with blood all over her.

JK: The following spring Alex got a letter addressed to "Mr. Alexander" from a lawyer, so I called my brother who said that all Alex had to do was send a certified letter to his insurance agent and tell him that a claim had been made against him. Homeowner's insurance. That took care of everything—they called us up when they got it and took a deposition over the phone. so the insurance company will pay her off to get rid of her, I guess, unless they check the blood tests they must have given her at the hospital.

AN: I'd had a feeling there was going to be a big problem with crashers that year because when I was on the subway that afteroon, I almost choked when I heard these two creeps sitting next to me say that the only good party that night was down on Prince and Lafayette! *My* place!!!

JK: At three in the morning at my own party, I didn't even know anybody I could bum a cigarette from.

AN: The next year was the year of what we've come to call the Phantom Ball. All year we were undecided about whether to continue the annual tradition and have a fourth Scarlet Ball, but by the fall we had decided not to. Then the *New York Times* called and said they wanted to do a story on the party that would run in their *Style* section right before New Year's. Well, for three years we'd been having the ball, just dying to get publicity in the *Times,* and now that we finally could get some press, I wasn't about to give it all up just because we weren't having the party! So I gave the interview and talked all about what the event was going to be like.

JK: It turned out to be their lead story. It said, "Russians Swirl in Soho."

AN: No, it said, "As Corks Pop on Sheik's Yacht in Harbor, Russian Aristocrats Swirl in Soho." As soon as it came out, a German TV crew wanted to come and film it—

JN: And a French one, too, and *Women's Wear* called and said they were going to have someone outside photographing the people coming in. And now different *departments* of the *Times* were calling—Food, Fashion, Real Estate—everything.

AN: And of course all my closest friends were insulted over why they hadn't been invited.

JK: And we couldn't admit we weren't having it, so when we would tell them, "No, you can't come," it just made them more determined to somehow get invited.

AN: The end result was I wound up staying home all New Year's Eve to make sure that nobody tried to break in.

How much help did you hire for your parties?

AN: For New Year's, all you have to drink is champagne, so we had two people contantly opening the bottles—at the end of the night their hands are bleeding. I actually impressed Sherry-Lehmann that last year when I ordered twenty-two cases: They went "Hmmm." And then you have two people cleaning up, and one person downstairs at the door; that's five. Plus our traditional doorman we hire for every one of our parties, Manny the Teacher. He's like a combination of Bobby Short and a butler from a Fred Astaire movie. He's a part-time teacher and he's great. So that's six. But the ideal ratio of help would be one-to-one—you've got to watch people.

JK: At one party I grabbed a girl who was leaving with one of my bas reliefs. I said, "Excuse me, where are you going with that?" She said, "I just wanted to see it in the elevator light." You have to take anything of value out of the rooms. Anything of possible perceived value. Which is everything. Ashtrays and flowers is all you leave. Take out any upholstered furniture, any rug. People at a party, drinking, they always forget they're in somebody's home and they'll put their cigarette out on the wall, whatever. People stand with their feet against the walls and it's a row of footprints.

JK: And the floor when it's over is like the foor of a porno theater. Alex wants to design a club, and for that, he'll draw on his experience from these parties.

AN: You have to ask youself, How can I make this place interesting and yet totally indestructible? It's a challenge to an architect.

DOORMEN

To have a freewheeling nightlife, by far the most crucial people to know are not the club owners or even celebrities—it's the men who work the doors. You don't need keys when you can jump start the car.

Six-foot-six doorman/performer-lyricist Dean Johnson is an imposing figure in some of New York's most discriminating doorways:

"I've been in New York seven years now. I went to college for four years and I wasn't part of the club scene then, even though I was right downtown at NYU. I couldn't get into any of the clubs, and anyway, I had no money. I remember when the Underground was really hot and we went up there one night and I watched the doorman do his thing and I thought, God, if you have to work, that's the job to have. It seemed like so much fun being up there and playing Caesar in a way. It seemed so glamorous to me. And also, getting in was my favorite part of going out. Once you got inside it wasn't that interesting anymore—I always just wanted to go out and try to get in again. For me, all the thrills are at the door. When I go to a club and get a no, then it's no. I'm not going to degrade myself by hanging around in the hopes of getting in. But there are people who really will. They'll holler and cry and try to bribe you. They'll go home and change clothes and try again. They'll tell you 'I work at NBC,' or 'I'm a waiter at——' hoping that what they do will somehow give them the status to get in. Or, My roommate's inside with the keys to our apartment.'

"After college I changed my whole look—I gave them all one they would want. I remember going to the Pyramid for the first time when I was still in school and my friend Holly and I were waiting for twenty minutes outside in the cold, and I was so naïve I didn't realize how arbitrary it was—I actually believed we were waiting for a space to be vacated inside the club so they would have room for us! I didn't realize they were picking and choosing. And when we finally got in, I felt so inadequate next to all these beautiful, avant-garde, underground people. Mann Parrish was playing. This was like, 1982.

"I remember looking at a copy of *Details* and seeing a picture of Dianne Brill jumping into the wading pool at Area. That made a big impression on me. I thought, My God, this woman doesn't really do anything, but if she ever does, with all this publicity, she'll start her career as a star. And I realized then how beneficial going out can be for a person in New York.

"I left NYU film school when I was a senior about to take finals, and I went to work at Boybar on St. Marks Place. That was 1983. I had done very well in school, but I got discouraged because I knew there were no jobs out there waiting for me.

"My first night on the door at Boybar I did Ecstasy. I didn't know what was going on. I was handling the door the way I thought it should

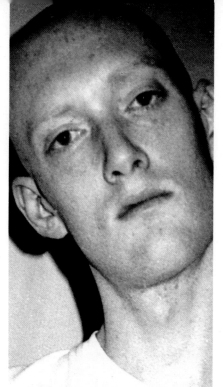

Doorman/rock performer Dean Johnson

be done, letting in people who I would like to meet in a club and keeping out the ones I wouldn't. And the manager came out and screamed at me, 'You're letting WOMEN in! This is BOYbar! No women!' I thought he was kidding, but he wasn't. He said, 'And no blacks and no Puerto Ricans.' I was like, shocked. I mean, my father's a minister, he marched with Joan Baez in civil-rights marches in the Sixties, and this was really antithetical to everything I believed in. But I needed the job so desperately that I said, 'Okay, I'll be a fascist.' So when these people would come to the door I would tell them, 'Look, the management doesn't want women, blacks, or Puerto Ricans in this nighclub.' And they freaked out, they couldn't believe I was being that honest with them. But I couldn't figure out any other way to do it, although I'd been told I should just tell them that there was no room inside. I was fired.

"That policy started to ruin the club—people wouldn't go there, they knew what was going on, and Boybar rapidly declined. Then the manager who had fired me was fired. He now works behind the cheese counter at a gourmet food store. And the owner never knew what had been going on; he'd been oblivious. Paul McGregor. He's this hairdresser from the Sixties who did the shag cut and made all this money doing Jane Fonda's and Julie Christie's hair.

"I did the door at a few more clubs and then Save the Robots opened on Avenue B. It started at two thirty A.M. and closed around seven-thirty in the morning. It was like a dream club—the kind of club I always imagined existed in New York. We opened right after Operation Pressure Point, which was when the police came down and swooped around on the open drug markets—spring of eighty-four. They did it because it was apparent the real-estate market was about to boom there, but the Lower East Side was still a rough place, the tourists didn't go there at all.

At Save the Robots you'd walk up to this old warehouse-looking building and then down in the basement you'd find two hundred of New York's most glamorous and exciting people. You'd have models and Rudolf and rich people, and skinheads and punks coming in off the street, and my friends, and I'd mix them all in. It was really fun; the atmosphere was just like a party. I never had a guest list the whole time I was there. If people I didn't want would show up at the door, I'd just say, 'You're at the wrong place.' I really don't like middle-class people who seem like they work in an office and go out at night looking for 'kicks.'

"I know it seems like discrimination to judge people on the basis of looks, but it's not, really, because they weren't born in those clothes—they went out and bought them. You can tell a person's personlity from his looks, if he's going to be fun or not. You're not looking for good looks so much as for fun. You have to be able to sum up a person's personality in a second, and I'm sure I make mistakes, but you have to. I know it's fascism and it's sick, but it's a living and I like it. I'm a very theatrical person and I see the door scene as theater. There's an audience there, looking for thrills, and if you entertain them while they're waiting to get in, you don't generate as much hostility. I'd always try to effect a great 'look' and put on a show for people so that even if they weren't getting in they were able to see a spectacle. So I'd usually be in drag. But in winter when it's cold, I'm usually not. If you don't have a bouncer, you have to just stick to your guns and pray to God that nobody *has* a gun. At Robots they could reach through the gates and grab at me, but at least there *was* a gate. It was iron and everybody would be outside looking at me.

"Because Robots was totally illegal, I could do whatever I wanted at the door—it was completely up to me who came in. I created a really nice atmosphere inside. And then the Fire Department came and closed us down and it took us a year and a half and fifty thousand dollars to get all the licenses we needed to reopen. And then we *thought* we were a legal club, but in order to be legal it had to be members-only, meaning people had to pay at the door, and it became very bureaucratic, the process of getting in, and it just ruined the fun and then we got busted anyway because they said we still didn't have the proper papers, and I went to jail and got really depressed seeing the way the police treated our customers. It was only a day in jail, but for a white boy like me from Massachusetts, that can be traumatic. I couldn't sleep for weeks. I quit and moved on to the World.

"Working at the World was the first time I'd ever worked in a legitimate club—it had a liquor license. I had lots of bouncers backing me up and so my life wasn't in danger dealing with people face to face in the street.

"Most of my real friends are people I knew long before I made the club scene—all people I met in college. The club scene is extremely superficial. I can't call any of the club people my 'friends.' They're great, but they're not people I would ever turn to in times of need. The only thing I love doing is my music. I want to be a pop star. I write all the music my group does. Lyrics are my strong point. I wrote one called 'Little Andy.'"

Fashion press agent Benjamin "Ming Vauze" Liu and artist Keith Haring. Right: Party-giver turned curator Baird Jones

Little Andy steelyard heat
Weak on a McKeesport street
Little Andy, sickly, meekly,
nervous breakdown semi-weekly.
Little Andy silver head
Lays it down on Mama's bed.

Little Andy come to town
Little Andy run around
Little Andy on the go
Little Andy one-man show
Little Andy everywhere
Little Andy millionaire.

Little Andy shopping spree
Cult of personality
Little Andy silver hair
Multiple electric chair.

Little Andy run around
Little Andy paint the town
Little Andy silver hair
Little Andy millionaire.

Little Andy piggy, greedy
Little Andy, where is Edie?
Little Andy standing nearer
Little Andy two-way mirror
Little Andy boy for me
Little Andy voyeur me
Little Andy stop my heart
Little Andy pop my art.

You don't want a homogenous crowd
inside a club, because people really do go
to nightclubs to make fun of the person
standing across the dance floor, so nobody's really happy if everybody in the
room looks the same as they do. You want
to get variety, which isn't always easy to
get. Being a doorman is not real life. It's
not a life and death situation. It's not
really important, so you take it all with a
grain of salt. You aren't really making de-
cisions yourself—those things are outlined
for you by the club you're working in at
the time. It's not real power. Anyone who
thinks it is is just mistaken.

**Veteran doorman/doyen/dilettante Haoui
Montaug (Hurrah, Danceteria, Palladium,
Tunnel, and more)**

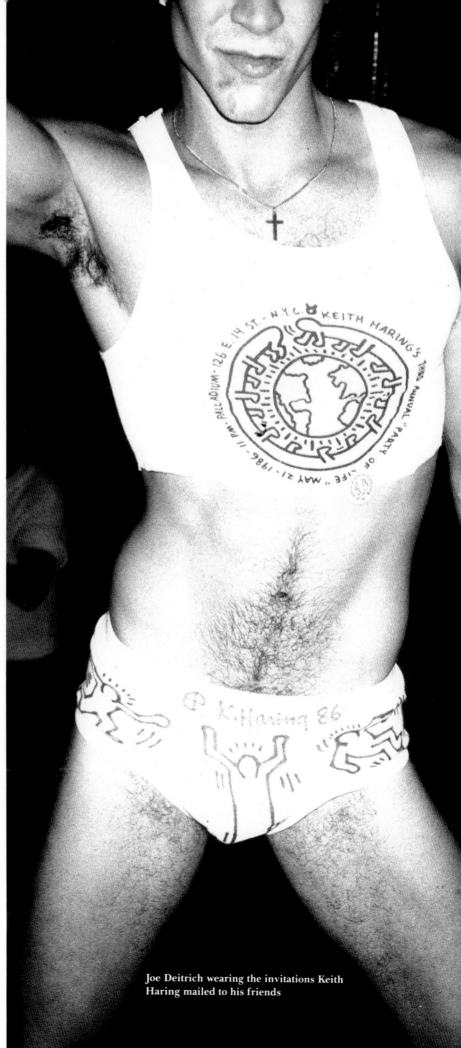

Joe Deitrich wearing the invitations Keith
Haring mailed to his friends

IMMOVEABLE DOORMEN

When art critic Edit deAk came to the United States from Albania in the late Sixties, she was hanging around with some of the NYU film school crowd. She couldn't speak English, so when they put her in an "underground" movie, Edit was supposed to scream, "THE REVOLUTION IS NOT A DINNER PARTY!" but she kept forgetting the "not." Today, she's in total command of the language and her following account shows how she was able to use it to (almost) negotiate her way through a door.

"I was at a party on West 10th Street at Duchamp's old house, and it wasn't far from Danceteria, so a friend and I walked up Fifth Avenue, drunk, with glasses of scotch in our hands. It was the night of a party there for a bunch of Japanese people I knew, but I had been eighty-sixed from the club a couple of weeks before because I'd told a carful of people to meet me there and the doorman rejected them. They were just nice, regular people, and I had a fight with him over that and I hadn't been back there since, so I had a feeling he was going to give me trouble this night, and he did, he wouldn't let me go in. I tried to persuade him and he wouldn't budge. I knew absolutely everybody inside this party, and it was so funny because as they were coming in and going out, they thought I had just come outside for some air, so they were all asking me how the party was. But this doorman had decided there was no way he was ever going to let me in. Even the owners came out to talk to him about it, but still he said no. Some people who had come out were trying to surround me and sneak me in, so then I played the honesty game with him. I said, 'Look. I could've sneaked in and I didn't,' and finally we were just at the point where we were talking one on one and soul to soul and he was giving in when somebody came out of the club and screamed at him, 'DON'T YOU KNOW WHO THIS IS?' And I waited, breathless, thinking that finally my American identity was going to come flashing for me. But then all he said was, 'THIS IS EDIT deAK!' The strain was finally too much. I went limp. Then I just left."

Sting and Dylan at Nell's

The black gloss door of Nell's can be one of New York's hardest to crack. Members and regulars sail through, but people not known to the two or three doormen or whose names aren't on the nightly lists they hold sometimes wait outside for hours hoping for the chance to either eat and drink on the main floor or dance and drink downstairs. Michael Smith—he's English—has worked the door there since opening night in the fall of 1986. "I'd worked for Rudolf at Danceteria, but not at the door," Michael told me. "Nell's is my first door job. Keith (McNally, the owner) took a chance on me—on *all* of us, really, including Nell—none of us had ever done before what we do here now." I asked Michael to tell me what nights at the door on West 14th Street are like:

"Your own tastes in people have to, obviously, agree somewhat with the aims of the club and the people you work for. If you follow your instincts, you tend not to make mistakes. I find the only time I make a mistake is if I second guess myself, if I think, 'Oh, I guess they're not really so bad,' and I let them in. I very rarely change my mind, though, because once you've made a decision, I don't think you should go back on it. . . . Yes, I do walk through the club periodically during the night to see how the mix looks, and yes, once in a while I'll think, 'How did I let it get this bad tonight?' When that happens, it's depressing, but it's usually your eye catching a couple of real eyesores, and that usually happens because

John Sex

(Baby) Jane Holzer and Milan

Dan Scheffey and Hollywood DiRusso

you've tried to be accommodating and you've let in extended groups: A regular, say, will show up with friends from out of town who want to see the place. I personally would never single out people in a group and say, 'You can come in, but you can't.' You don't want to offend anyone—especially the regular who's brought them, so you try to be subtle and say something like, 'We probably won't have room for your *whole* group tonight.' If the person's smart they sort of know what you mean.

"You can't put your finger on what it is that makes you want to have a person in the club. It's different things with different people. With some it's youth and energy and danceability, the way they're dressed or extreme beauty. With other people it's something less obvious, a kind of intelligence. People can be not particularly chic or stylish, but if they have a good manner, they're good material.

"When in doubt what to wear, I guess black is a wonderful thing, even if it's somewhat unimaginative. People in Los Angeles must have a totally different way of dressing to go out at night, because I find that most of the people who're nightmares fashion-wise inevitably say to me, 'But I've just come from L.A....'

"Occasionally people will call up and say a celebrity is coming and then those people will come, but without the celebrity, and that's embarrassing, because you have to sort of say, *(laughs)* 'Where is the celebrity?' I hate people who trade on other people's celebrity. I think it's really sick, don't you? If you're so insecure you won't use your own name and personality to get in somewhere, I think it's really depressing."

I asked Michael if he'd like to continue on in this job and maybe become a long-term classic figure at the Nell's door, and he said without missing a beat, "Oh, I think so, yes, if this turns out to be the classic place I think it will." In contrast to Michael, who once took two years off to go back to England and study *philosophy,* another doorman at Nell's, Jessica Rosenblum, took a

year off from school to do *PR-for-real-estate.* She's still only twenty-one, and hasn't made her "academic decision on whether to finish Columbia." Jessica told me:

"I'd just been hanging around the club scene when I was a full-time student, and I was here the night Nell's opened. I was very decked out and socializing to the max and obviously knew everybody and Keith saw me and offered me a job. I waitressed for about two months and then they put me on the door. People have all different approaches when they come up to the ropes, but some of them are really excessive and say things like, 'You stupid bitch, is this all you do for a living? See where it's going to get you.' The only thing Nell and Keith feel strongly about is being polite. I think we're the only door in New York that bothers to explain to people why they're not getting in so they don't waste their evening. If somebody's really inappropriate for the club, I tell them the same line I do when we actually *are* overcrowded. I say, 'We need to save room for our members.'

"This is definitely not my career. Of course, I would definitely like to own a bar or be a partner in a restaurant, but I don't see that as a *career.* Basically, I want to act, I want to be in movies. This is fun, it's like my seventeen-year-old fantasy, when I clubbed everywhere but didn't know anybody, and now I get to know everybody and everybody gets to know me.

"I don't go crazy when I see celebrities. My father is the executive director of one of the top regional theaters in America where a lot of prestigious people perform so I was in that milieu and it was always, like, 'Oh, Vincent Price is coming to the house for dinner.' I don't want to sound blasé, but that's the way I was brought up. But what *was* sort of fun was, say, when Faye Dunaway came in. She's just *so* brilliant at the door, being like a total movie star but *so* nice and there were a couple hundred people outside and she got out of her limo in this outfit that was to die and sunglasses and the crowd went hush, and I've *never*

seen that happen, and that's just what makes your night fun because there's a certain thrill of seeing somebody being great with their position.

"On my nights off I usually wind up here because this is where all my friends hang out. The mix we have here is the best in any club in New York in a long time."

I asked Michael how he prepares himself mentally to accept and reject people all night every night, if his philosophy studies helped at all: "No, no, you just have to be totally professional about it. Rejecting people can be very depressing, sometimes. If you get too emotionally involved you can't do your job properly. But what makes it all rewarding is when people tell you on the way out that they've had a great time, that the club is great. And the nice thing about making the door quite difficult is that once people do get inside, they seem to feel like they're in one big VIP room so they strike up converstions more easily."

With its drawing-room atmosphere—low lighting, oriental rugs, and random upholstered couches, love seats, and club and wing chairs, Nell's hit on a common denominator look that every different age and type of person seems comfortable in. You feel like you're hanging around some sort-of-rich person's sort-of-English house and that they've gone away and left it for you and your friends to have fun in. Nell's filled the void left recently by people giving parties in clubs and restaurants instead of in the places where they live—at Nell's club, you *do* feel like you're just lounging. Nell told me, "My own apartmen' looks exactly like the club, and it's turned out that because the club looks like a private house, people treat it better. When I used to visit New York in the Seventies, the Mudd Club was my favorite place, and I noticed there that when you have a concrete floor, people do tend to, of course, put their cigarettes out on it. Whereas here we've made our dance floor look like we just pulled back the rug so the kids can dance on the floorboards, just the way you would at a party at home."

Nell Campbell

NELL

I met Nell Campbell in London in the late Seventies at a great party Ann Lambton gave for me. Nell was in a Vivian Westwood pink rubber outfit and her hair was shocking pink, too. She sang a song on a marble staircase and she was just great. Since she opened her club in New York she hasn't performed in it (except one song on New Year's), but I think she should.

Do you consider yourself a hostess here?

I still think of myself as an actress—a comedienne, I suppose, that being the work I've done since I was eighteen. And being an actress is helpful for me in doing this role here every night, because every night I dress in totally different ways, and that's what keeps it interesting for me.

Do all the designers give you free clothes and ask you to wear them in the club?

No. I will tell you right now that Calvin Klein is the first person to ever *give* me a dress, and I think he's an absolute doll for it! Now that he's broken the spell, I hope and pray that everyone else will follow his example.

What about acting jobs? Do the celebrities who come here offer you any movie roles?

Oh, you never get jobs from your friends. That's something I learned very early on.

THIS EVENT IS BEING FILMED AND MAY BE EXHIBITED COMMERCIALLY WORLD WIDE IN ALL MEDIA IN PERPETUITY. BY YOUR APPEARANCE HERE TODAY YOU CONSENT TO YOUR APPEARANCE IN THE PROGRAM AND EXCERPTS THEREOF.

The New York opening of a Playboy Club

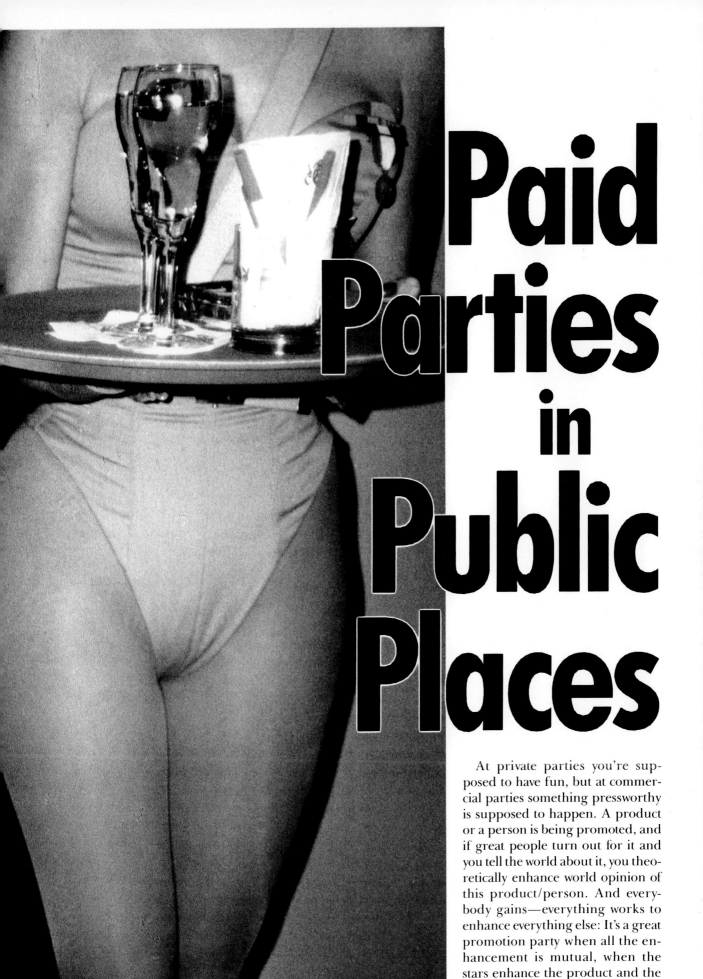

Paid Parties in Public Places

At private parties you're supposed to have fun, but at commercial parties something pressworthy is supposed to happen. A product or a person is being promoted, and if great people turn out for it and you tell the world about it, you theoretically enhance world opinion of this product/person. And everybody gains—everything works to enhance everything else: It's a great promotion party when all the enhancement is mutual, when the stars enhance the product and the product enhances the stars, when

Michael Douglas, Yoko Ono, "Jezebel,"
and Jann Wenner smoking. Below:
Albums at the place setting at a dinner
given by King's record company

everyone's success rubs off on everyone else's.

After you've been in public life for a while, you can take anybody you want to a party and still get noticed, but if you're just starting out and want to make a splash and have a flash thrown your way when you arrive, you have to take a beauty to a party. Most beauties are trouble—you have to call them forty times, you go nuts trying to confirm if they're going or not, and if they are, will they go with you or are they looking for somebody better who they'll drop you for at the last second, etc. No question about it, a stunning date on your arm really does the trick, but these beauties will make you a nervous wreck. Eighties girls are much less spoiled than Sixties and even Seventies girls were; Eighties girls will meet you at the place, and some of them even have a car and will pick *you* up. An alternative to taking a beauty is taking someone who's wild-looking in some way—your Mr. Ts, your Liberace-types, your John Sexes. Eye-catchers like these would all be someone you could get press with and avoid all the waiting you usually have to do for the sensational women.

Everybody who goes to a lot of press parties learns how to do their one or two good angles for the cameras—those couple of poses they look good in—and that's why you see all the pros looking pretty much the same at every party: They've figured out which poses don't make them look like a dope, which it's so easy to look like in a picture that's taken three inches from your face with a flash. Practice in a mirror, find those angles.

When they're at promotional parties, celebrities are on their most professional behavior, because they've psyched themselves up for the public. They know they've got to do whatever they can to make the public happy, and therefore this is a great moment to get a picture of yourself with them, if your timing is right. Their mind-set is one of accommodation, so if you just maneuver your way to the center of the party—i.e., right next to that hardworking star—and if you have one

or, for insurance, two friends with instant-focus cameras covering your progress and waiting for your magic moment, you can come away from the event with a photo you'll cherish for a lifetime. If you go out to events a lot, you'll probably have become friends with a few of the professional photographers who cover them all, so you know that you can always recruit them to do you a favor, give you some backup. You have to be very quick, though, and throw yourself into the celebrity's arms before they get a chance to wonder if they know you or not. They are working, so for a few moments they'll just consider this part of their job, until they get a second thought about it, and by this time, you've gotten away with what you need. (*Need* is the crucial word. Always tell a celebrity that you "need" a picture, never that you "want" one—it carries more weight.)

(And by the way, the truly classy celebrity will always make sure that his/her expression looks even more thrilled to be with you than you are to be with them.)

Donny Osmond

ROCK-AND-ROLL PARTIES

Danny Fields is currently a radio producer. He's been on both sides of the rock-and-roll party story—in the Sixties when he worked for record companies he gave the events, and then when he began writing columns for newspapers and magazines, he went from being the courter to the courted. I had this talk with him in the spring of eighty-six, at the height of a mega-party in the maxi-club phase of nightlife.

You look great.

Thank you. It's because I don't go to a lot of parties. It's not a beauty regimen, going to parties. It's unnatural to sleep away the daylight hours waiting to go out at night, to be in rooms full of smoke, drugs, and alcohol fumes. It takes a visible toll. The very young can go out night after night with impunity, but as soon as they're over twenty-five, party people start to turn a certain color; it's not a human you.

How have rock parties changed over the years?

The bottom fell out of the whole thing in the mid-Seventies. It used to be fabulous. I remember once they flew a planeload of us from London to New York for a party for a band I can't remember the name of now, and I'm sure no one else can, either. Flew them back the next day. That was what it used to be like. Susan Blond once flew us to Denmark for dinner to see a band. I came back and never heard of them again. Of course I wrote something, I had my column in the *Soho News* then: "I had a divine trip to Copenhagen to see————, the biggest thing in Denmark." Where a "gold record" means they sold 750 albums. In about 1970 they hired me and Lisa Robinson to give a party in that restaurant that was all silver, on East 59th Street, or 58th. Right off the Park, sort of where the Savoy Plaza was, where the airlines ticket office is, and it was all brand new and stainless steel and about three floors and they told us, "Give a party for The Who, but please don't go over twenty thousand dollars. Nothing elaborate, just make it nice." We could do whatever we wanted. That's unheard of now. If I didn't go to the Rainbow Room for a buffet dinner after a concert at least once a week, it wasn't a week. You did not have to budget food into your life. If you were in the rock press corps, even if you were a third-level C-list person, your life was taken care of with these parties. And that's all we talked about: "How was the shrimp at Led Zeppelin?" "Oh, the lobster at Atlantic was better than at Warner Brothers." This was our conversation.

Music business regulars Linda Stein, Danny Fields, and Dean Zimmerman, plus Rudolf

After Woodstock, once we got all that share-the-wealth hippie nonsense over with, everyone just dug right in. There was so much money, they didn't know what to do with it. The glory days were from about 1970 to seventy-five or seventy-six, and then the bottom fell out—people learned how to tape copies or whatever happened.

Rock parties started out pretty small, though, in the Sixties.

Right. That's when I was working for record companies, so I was giving the parties. The record world was so much smaller then that you could get away with a party for The Doors in some middle-level restaurant in midtown for like three thousand dollars and everybody would be happy. Later, after I'd left Elek-

tra and budgets started to soar, they gave a party for The Doors in the penthouse duplex at the New York Hilton. Remember? The food was fantastic, you had Jim Morrison wandering around, and the view was incredible! What more could you ask for? That's a perfect example of the kinds of parties we got used to—expensive and up-there. I mean, if you did not have a view, you *complained*. You wanted to know that you were, one, in New York and, two, on at least the forty-eighth floor of *something*. You'd usher the group over to the window looking out over the city so you could tell them, "Welcome to New York—it's at your feet." New York, high up, with the carpet of lights—that's how it was done. Today they shove you onto barges or drag you down

into basements or pull you into conference rooms and tell you you're having a party. Although that party for Dolly Parton that we went to on top of the World Trade Center a few years ago was really special. When nobody else was up there. And all Windows on the World food. Her record company did that for her, and it was great.

Yeah, that was fun.

I guess the people coming into the business now are unspoiled; they have no expectations, they don't know what life used to be like. There was always a party for the first time a group arrived in New York, then for the second time they arrived, parties for every concert—there were parties not just for every contract signing, but for every ini-

Sam Bolton and Shelly Fremont with a ZZTop on board the MTV boat

tialing of every clause! Mind you, I don't know what the record companies thought this would accomplish. Whoever was telling them that having these parties was essential—well, I shouldn't say "whoever" because it was people like me and Lisa and Lillian Roxon who got them into this consciousness, but it's amazing that they believed what we were telling them! Everybody saw that everybody was happy, and I guess they began to figure that the more they spent, the more wonderful it would be and the more good would rub off on their group. I don't think they ever correlated it scientifically to an increase in record sales, but there was enough money then to budget for all this "good will." However, when the companies began to cut back, this

Nick Ashford and Valerie Simpson

Dolly Parton at a dinner to celebrate changing labels

Architect Peter Marino and writer Steven M.L. Aronson at Roseland

was the first totally dispensable item they saw.

One of the first parties I can remember where the record company paid to promote a group was the one you did at Max's—

Yeah, in sixty-six to promote Cream, Atlantic Records gave us a budget of four hundred dollars. It was a breakfast at Max's Kansas City.

Lately the record companies are just giving parties in the big clubs.

Yeah, the irony is that the record companies have become just another one of the many kinds of institutions that use the computer lists of the discotheques for parties. And do you know what these huge clubs do when it's an "open bar" and the drinks are free? Well, here's their strategy for that: They hire one palsied, spastic, deaf, blind bartender to dispense the free drinks so that yes, indeed, if, with five hundred people squashing you to death, you can attract the attention of this vegetable, you will get a free drink. I mean, forget about drinking—you want to take up a collection and send him to a home! But then, at the stroke of midnight when they switch over to "cash bar," in runs the Olympic bartending team who can all take six orders while they pour twelve drinks with one hand and make change with their feet.

Do you have any tips for young people just starting out in the world of rock-and-roll party-going?

Yes, I'll share something I learned the first week I came to New York. It was true then and it's true now: Rooms are controlled by the people sitting at tables. This goes for parties and for bars and restaurants where you hang out. If you're standing and being buffeted and you don't know where you're going to be the next second, you have no control over the flow of events as they pertain to you at this party. No matter what your ends are—social, business, sexual— you've got to be in a strategic place in order to steer the world. A chair has always been symbolic of

Joey Arias

power—the throne, the Oval Office—the *seat* of power. Even at parties, chaotic as they are, all the more reason to have a base of operations to keep people away, to bring them toward you. No one knows this better than Lisa Robinson and Fran Lebowitz. Especially Lisa. And for the right reasons. Because there aren't that many tables, and once you have yours, you have your beachhead. This is the first axiom

of partygoing.

Do you ever get up from the seat?

Watch Lisa and you'll see that she never gets up to say hello—she'll signal. Unless it's, say, her party for Mick Jagger and Mick walks in; then she'll get up. But otherwise she'll hold that table. And when people approach she'll either wave them over and indicate they should sit down, or she'll give them the nod

that means, "Keep walking, keep walking." Like at any party.

But what if you get there real late and there's no chance for a table?

What I do is stand there and I begin putting out very fragile, infirm vibrations, like, "I am a very delicate person and I do not come here very often"—these Queen Mother vibrations. And someone inevitably picks up on them and says, "Is there

Barbie doll collector BillyBoy* with Barbie fans at the New York opening of his touring Barbie collections

anything I can do for you? Can I go get you a drink?" "Yes indeed, son, you can." Like I can barely stand up; meanwhile I'm at the gym working out for a couple of hours a day.

Is there any etiquette for a rock-and-roll party?

There are no niceties, really. Let's remember we're talking about a bunch of slobs. I'm sure that when,

say, Mica Ertegun is hostessing a rock-and-roll party, her expectations of formality are considerably different from when she's doing one of her society-fashion-charity-type things. Mica has a wonderful instinct for how to be herself, but still preside over a rock-and-roll party. She adjusts instinctively and instantly to the needs of the moment, which is the definition of a true rock-and-roll hostess. Remember when Ahmet and Mica actually threw open their Upper East Side house to a rock party—they let TV cameras in and everything? Then after the crews left, the whole party ran upstairs to watch ourselves on the eleven o'clock news.

How do you feel about music at parties?

If a party's for a group that's in town to promote their record, I think it's in very bad taste to play that particular record at the party for them.

Really? Why?

If you were at a party for a writer, would you pass copies of his book all around the room and have people stand there reading it? No. So why play their music? And inevitably the music is either so loud you can't talk to people, which is rude to all the guests, or it's so low you don't notice it anyway, which is rude to the group, because it's using it as background music. In other words, this great artistic effort—the result of people standing around a studio for months worrying about which knob to turn and spending incredible amounts of money for things that only they hear and no one else cares about—is now being used as Muzak!

Isn't it amazing how much time people spend in studios now working on albums? Years, sometimes!

Please, it's like a riddle: If you spend a year in the studio making a really good album, what do you get if you spend *two* years? A really *really* good album? Have you ever been to a listening party?

What's that?

Where the record company actu-

ally debuts the record before your very ears? You sit there and they're all lined up and there's nothing to look at, so you avert your eyes and look at the wall while they scrutinize you to see if you're tapping your feet or what. Sometimes there's a bowl of fruit on the side, but otherwise this is a serious gathering. Believe me, you would rather be in a midnight fire at sea.

One of Susan Blond's first jobs in New York was selling ads for our magazine, Interview. *She left us in the early Seventies to go work at United Artists Records, and that was the start of her career in record-industry publicity. Throwing parties for her label's artists is only a small part of a publicist's job, but it's the part, she says, that causes the most problems. (See the next chapter for an account of the landmark Michael Jackson party she organized in 1984.) Now she's president of Susan Blond, Inc., a public relations company that specializes in music, but when we had this conversation she was vice president of media relations at Epic Records, which is part of CBS.*

What was the first record party you threw?

The first party I did was while I was at United Artists—for Electric Light Orchestra. I had a budget of two hundred fifty dollars and I threw it at the City Squire Hotel and invited all the fanzine writers and all the high-school and college paper writers. In order to get everyone into a state of excitement, when the group walked in I started yelling, "Here they come! Here they come!" And I began sort of attacking the group myself, hoping that everyone else would follow. That was very low budget, but it was effective—we got the press we wanted.

You threw some lavish parties, too.

Oh, yeah. When I started at CBS in seventy-four we would throw parties at places like the Rainbow Grill and the Tower Suite for twenty-five, thirty thousand dollars—they would stop at nothing. There was a Procol Harum party at the Plaza, I remember, which was the first time all the rock-and-rollers wore tuxedos. I hate to admit it, but that one was given by Warner Brothers. Until then they were all just in a very sloppy mode—they'd never even been in a suit and tie, most of them. It didn't start a trend, though. To this day, in rock and roll, most people rent their tuxedos. It's never been a very formal business. The day before I started working at Epic, by the way, they did Sly Stone getting married in Madison Square Garden. Remember that?

When did the parties start to get small again?

About six years ago I became a vice president here at CBS. I had at one point thirty-five people working for me. Now I have two in New York and two in L.A. It was small when I began, and then it got very big, and now it's small again. Something happened and the record industry got huge and peaked. It didn't grow anymore, thanks to home taping or video games, whatever did it. It's a miracle I've survived.

At one point there we flew a bunch of writers to see Sailor and Boxer, and then over to Denmark for dinner to see Gasolin.

I love all those Seventies names.

Right. And there was one person who never wrote a word about the trip, and I never forgave him. I mean, after a trip like *that* you *better* write about it! It's unspoken . . .

Anyway, those were the days when we would spare no expense. We went from that to trying to put parties together in the *(laughs)* conference room and doing "creative" things to decorate. Like when we got Slim Whitman on our label? He was known for his yodeling and so we threw hay all over the conference room.

I like Slim Whitman—why wasn't I invited?

I didn't know you did. You see, he had sold a lot of records through mail-order ads on TV, and we thought we could sell more through a record company, but we were wrong *(laughs)*. *His* campaign worked and ours didn't.

What was that party you did at the Planetarium?

That was for Hawkwind.

Who?

H-a-w-k-w-i-n-d. One word. They were an English band, and a woman with a forty-inch chest used to dance naked as part of the rock and roll, and they made very spacy music, so we did it at the Planetarium. When we had our Adam Ant party at the Ritz, nobody could get in. People with invitations were outside because the place was packed to capacity. Parties are enormous work and they bring you enormous trouble. There are still restaurants I can't get a table in, and people who still won't return my phone calls because I did not invite them to the Michael Jackson party. That will follow me my whole life. Because that party was so huge, and yet I still had to say no to hundreds of people. The first party I did for Culture Club was at Mr. Chow's, and there were at least six hundred people on the list, but Mr. Chow's only held one hundred fifty. So I started calling my best friends and asking them did they really want to come, and wasn't it awfully cold out and wouldn't it be boring, anyway? These people have never gotten over being *dis*invited.

I always try to get a restaurant or a club to do a free party—do it just for the publicity, you know? So early on in Boy George's career I hooked up with some of the royalty around town because I thought their names would get me this free party at Mr. Chow's. However, I wound up paying in full for the party, and the royalty ended up sitting at the good table and getting the free champagne, while Boy George and all my bosses were stuck at the bad tables. Plus, my bosses were not impressed with royalty at all, either before or after that party. Stevie Winwood and Jann Wenner were there. And *(laughs)* Mr. Chow still remembers how I begged him not to charge me per head for the dinners: "Sure six hundred people came, but they didn't all *eat!* And look at all the *tastemakers* we brought in!"

New York harbor during the Statue of Liberty celebration in 1986

BILLYBOY*: BARBIEBOY

BillyBoy* has the world's largest collection of Barbie dolls. Mattel sponsored a tour of America and Europe for a show Billy created where hundreds of Barbies were dressed in the couture outfits that he had great fashion designers make up especially for her. They were displayed in glass cases while Barbie commercials from the Sixties played on TV monitors. In New York, the show was installed at one of the huge pier buildings, and the opening party felt as if Barbie herself had done the guest list, because it was such an odd mix—Mattel employees in their company blazers were mixed in with all the downtown people and the New York press corps and the regular Barbie fans.

What are the advantages of having a Barbie party?

You sit at home and place your dolls around you and at least you know that everyone at your party will be well dressed. And with your dolls positioned around you, you can always be the center of attention. You can artificially get a sense of power because you're so much bigger than they are, and when you want to pick somebody up, you just literally pick them up and put them in your pocket. And you won't ever be embarrassed because you say the wrong thing, because everything you need to know about Barbie is written on the side of her box—you can't go wrong.

That's when Barbie comes to your world for a party. What about when she goes to a party in her own?

"It's a Barbie World!" Just different perspectives on the same thing. Every day's a party for Barbie. When you have neat clothes to wear, you create occasions to wear them, even if it's inside the intimacy of your own toy chest. Barbie gives parties for Midge—at least, that's what the TV commercial said in 1963. And one night she gave a masquerade. And we know she's a great hostess because she has "entertaining outfits" called Golden Evening and Golden Glamour. And there's that persimmon strapless capri jumpsuit with a gold net hostess coat. I mean, where else would you wear that except to entertain friends at home?

Who does Barbie invite to her parties?

She doesn't have to worry about whether friends will show up or not, because they're usually right there in the same Barbie Doll case. She doesn't discriminate—she likes to invite all kinds of people. The problem at most parties is that people want to invite only cool people, and that's so boring. That's like segregation. Barbie knows how to invite everyone and they all have a good time because Barbie sets the tone.

Does Barbie go to other people's parties?

She's the perfect guest. She doesn't drink because she doesn't have a mouth that opens. She won't fill up the room with cigarette smoke. She always arrives on time, she can help you with the last-minute preparations, and if you want her to go home early she doesn't mind—she takes it well. Like when you're real tired and you yawn? She understands. Barbie would also understand if you didn't invite her.

"Bachelor of the Year" carpenter Glen Lyons surrounded by left to right Anita Sarko, Dianne Brill, Dinah Prince, and Janice Savitt (beneath an unidentified hat-wearing admirer)

Supermodel Kim Alexis

Carol is a secretary at a recording studio. She goes to Alcoholics Anonymous, and I talked to her about parties without liquor.

What do you do at parties now that you're in AA?

Sober partying is different. But the AA dances are good. There's a club downtown called the NOW club that's on St. Marks Place in the old Electric Circus building.

What does "NOW" mean?

I don't know. Something to do with not being an alcoholic.

Do you want to meet new men when you go to these dances?

I have a boyfriend, Arthur, but I rarely see him—just a couple of times a week. So I go to these dances and I get duded up—tight jeans and a top and high heels and what have you. I like long baths before I go out. They really relax me. Then I wash my hair and then I set it because I love curls. I gotta look good in order to have a good time. What I like about going to these NOW dances is that the music is definitely disco. Black disco. When I dance I really get into it—the movements, the music, the feeling in the room. . . . The people there are recovering alcoholics, recovering drug addicts, and a lot of them don't know yet how to dance sober. I'm learning how to do that and I really enjoy it. I come home exhausted. And of course I do get sexually aroused, because the people are very sleazy there. There's some kind of sleazy arousal about them—like you can imagine while you're dancing that you're in bed with them or something? And you groove with certain movements. It's basically a dance hall with a wooden floor like a gym. I love to laugh and I love to dance. I'm a very good dancer—high kicks and jumps and what have you.

Do you ever make business contacts at parties?

No. Parties are just to have fun.

Have you ever been to any singles-type parties?

Yes, and I'll tell you why. Arthur

Writer Michael Musto

Scott Cohen and magazine editor Gael Love

Playboy rabbit Robert Mailhouse and
Hollywood exec Susan Pile

started seeing this twenty-two-year-old baby who lives with her parents. What more can you say, you know? So my mother—good Jewish mother—said, "Go out and meet some guys." She had lost my father in May and in the mail she would get this what's-going-on-for-singles magazine. There was one party for twenty-seven dollars, and this other one that said, "Only twelve dollars with this invitation. Men wear jackets, no jeans." So I went. I wore this mini-dress and even gold makeup—I didn't know that it was the straightest thing in the world. You walked into this townhouse and there's a bar with free drinks. I had three seltzers. All the women were Jewish secretaries. I mean, I'm a Jewish secretary, but *these* . . . And the music was terrible; they were doing everything from meringue to bop, and this accountant comes over and says, "I don't even dance here because people don't know how." So we left the dance floor and there's couches all over with little candles, and oh, Lord! I left so fast with this guy that they must've thought I was making money or something, I don't know. They gave me a "look" . . . So I looked at him and said, "So what do we do now? Go to bed with each other?" I'm telling you, this guy was *happy!* But that's not what happened. We did go to my apartment, but I developed a cabaret act for him. I sang for two hours.

Did he sing, too?

No, he just watched. Then I got tired, so I finally did have sex with him. I was so in shock over my boyfriend leaving me. People who know Arthur and me say we'll be forever. Of course, I can't tell him that because he'll get nervous. Anyway, that was a bad party. They kept sending me invitations. Forget it. I'm used to good-looking men. I've always had handsome men in my life. Macho, sex-appeal men. This guy wasn't great, but he was the best of a bad situation. And at these singles parties, when they say forty people, figure it means, like, twelve.

Alan Rish is a "party-giver/actor" which, as he explains it, is "one step above a waiter/actor."

Photographer Robert Mapplethorpe

How did you get into the party business?

Cornelia Guest, the DuPont twins, and I all interned with Nikki Haskell. We'd go to the printer's and make phone calls and work on guest lists while Nikki was off in Brazil or going to Charles Jourdan and buying fifty pairs of shoes. The DuPonts would sleep all day, but they thrived on the phone, and

Leach, they're no more or less ridiculous than Nikki.

When did you begin doing your own parties?

I started with Rudolf at Danceteria. That's where I made all my mistakes. He would keep telling me, "You have no street-smarts—you love everybody." But he doesn't tell me that anymore, because you

level. There's a real level, and then a little less real and then a little less, until you get to the level where you just wave across the room. If you can't even bring yourself to wave at them, it's over.

How does a party at a club come about?

You usually come up with the idea for a party and then you tell the club, "I have a fabulous party for so-and-so," and hope they'll go for it. For Jermaine Jackson at the Limelight our budget ws really good. Like eighty thousand dollars we ended up spending. From the invitations to the messengers. The club paid most of it because they wanted it splashy. But the record company paid some. That came from Clive Davis. The more a club wants a party, the more they're willing to spend.

What has your career done for your own personal popularity?

Throwing parties opens lots of doors, but you've got to be careful not to push it. Presidents of companies answer your calls immediately because they know you're just going to invite them to something. But once you get them to come, it'd better be good. The idea is to do really earth-shattering parties where people are still talking about it a week later and not just forgetting it by later that night. And it's great when everyone calls the next day and tells how upset the people who didn't come were when they heard how good it was. Of course you do have occasional fiascoes. Sometimes people will come up to me in the middle of a party and say, "Oh, Alan, this is like *bad.*" It happens.

Author Tama Janowitz

Cornelia was fun but flighty. I worked for free for credit for school. Nikki was then doing parties at the Underground to pay for her cable TV show. She would get the celebrities to come to the Underground for dinner, film them there, and then the Underground would pay for the production costs of her show. If she'd had more luck, she could have made it big on TV. When you look at Dr. Ruth or Robin

finally get an instinct. At first, anybody that looked good or was fun or witty, I would think—fabulous. But you begin to discern differences and you separate the people who are not really good. You still invite them, but you cut it off sharply at some level. And as for friends, you literally have five or six good friends who you'll go meet the next afternoon for breakfast, and the rest are just people on another

How do you get paid?

I usually try for a flat fee. It depends. If you have a tremendous star, you go for the most you can. But money doesn't motivate me—fabulousness does. The only way you can survive doing what I do is if you only do things that are special with beautiful, talented people. I think the time for weirdness is past already. What I want to do next is something truly elegant, but not uptight. You know the white parts

Mr. and Mrs. Neil Simon at Sardi's after a
Broadway opening

Elizabeth Taylor and her mother

of Versailles? Not the gilt parts, but the very white and classical parts? With the moldings and everything? That's the kind of place I would like. But with no rules—just be fabulous. I do think this party-giving will lead to something else. It hasn't yet, but my life has always been ruled by fate, it'll all just come.

Who do you put on your guest list?

Someone who's distinctive in some way or another. Beauty, fame, heritage, money, fun, creativity—

Good character?

I'm not looking for good character, no. I mean, I'm not a church looking to conscript people for heaven. Fortunately, you don't have to deal with moral issues when you're having parties.

Describe your typical day.

I try never to wake up before twelve. My day is half very glamorous, half very not. Like when I have a mailing to do and have to sit there and really scrutinize the list and then paste labels by hand. That takes five hours. When you design an invitation, you have to go to the artists, work with them, go to the typesetter's and proof it—you do it all yourself, nothing can be left to chance. You have to be able to relate to printers and waiters and busboys and security men as well as to princesses and writers and artists and disco owners. You try to work with

people who understand what you're trying to accomplish, otherwise there's going to be trouble—people getting offended. I remember working so hard to get Jeremy Irons to come to one particular party. He was so hot on Broadway at that moment, and he's so fabulous, and I was expecting him. I was running back and forth all night from the party to the door, making sure everything was running right, and around midnight I arrive at the door and see Jeremy Irons getting *into* a taxi in front of the club. Before I could get to him the cab pulled away and I turned to the doorman and started screaming, "That was JEREMY IRONS! How could you turn him away!" And this big bruiser says, "Hey, take it easy—it's not like it was Frank Sinatra."

Have you done any big corporation parties?

A few, and they're great because they give you so much money to work with, you can really do a lot. I did one for Z-100 radio station and they flew Pia Zadora in. Actually, she flew herself in. At that point she was a joke, like Cher used to be. But she's talented and she's becoming a nonjoke.

Do you have fun at your own parties?

Definitely. I get so excited. And if I'm at a really great party and it's not mine, I get so jealous. Vito

Bruno had a party on the Williamsburg Bridge for Annie Flanders. You could see the subway go by and everything shook and it was fabulous. Fun people were there and it was just such a scene. I said, "Oh, shit, I wish this were mine."

How do you get publicity for your parties?

I don't believe in PR agents. Something's either going to be publicized or it isn't. I wouldn't hound somebody to hound, say, Liz Smith or Suzy to write about me—I mean, whenever the time's right, they'll put me in.

What's your professional goal?

This is a scary business. I see no role models who are in positions that I would like to end up in. I mean, I only see wrecks of humanity who used to do what I do. I don't want to do this forever. I always go back to this: It's not forever. It can't be forever. Something has to result from this. It has to lead to something. I'm taking acting lessons now, but I hate "actors," really—I love movie stars because that's a whole different breed. But real working Broadway actors are the worst. All they talk about is "craft" and they have deep voices and they're horrible, you know? Eventually, I want to be a movie star. "A socialite/party-giver, and now he's in a movie." I *know* I could get all the press.

Ted Guefen and Bettina

PROMOTING A CLUB, NOT A FAMILY

The problem one publicist had when he organized a party for the opening of a downtown club is one that all party promoters face.

"The owner of the club had hired me to make sure it was a glamorous opening, all the right, great-looking, fun people. So what does he do? He invites all his relatives from Long Island, and I was dying! They looked—from Great Neck. I said to him, 'Richard. This is *business*. You are the owner, but it's not Family Night! Why can't you understand it's for your benefit to have nothing but fabulous people here? If you bought *Vogue* magazine, would you want your relatives to start modeling all the clothes?' So he disinvites his relatives, but what he doesn't tell me is that he's also invited the investors, and when *these* tacky people started walking in the door, I absolutely had a heart attack. I screamed, 'Richard! Get them out! Right now!' He's saying, 'But they're the *investors.*' I said, 'I don't care. Just have them come back on another night or there'll be nothing to invest in but a disaster!'"

WHO'S COMING

Professional party-giver Nikki Haskell says that it's a dilemma knowing how much to tell the press.

"When you think that a certain celebrity is coming, if you tell the press that he's expected and then he doesn't show up, you've ruined the party and you're the bad guy. On the other hand, if you *don't* tell them and he *does,* you're the bad guy again because they missed him. You're caught in the middle. The dilemma is huge when the star is huge, because emotions are running so strong and the press at stake is major. I gave a party for Yul Brynner at Studio 54 once, and I was 90 percent certain Michael Jackson was coming, but I didn't want to say so in case he didn't and everyone would be disappointed. I was looking at my watch every three seconds, and I sent someone over to the West Side to get the special orange and carrot and apple juice that he drinks. I didn't tell anyone I was expecting him, but when he finally did come, I was so exhausted from all the will he?/won't he? that I almost collapsed with relief."

Professional party-giver Nikki Haskell

There is a position half-way between owning a club yourself and being a professional party organizer with a mailing list: Ludovic Autey runs the Junior International Club and Marc Biron has Club Biron. Both were born in France and their "clubs" in New York consist of members who pay an annual fee. Ludovic and Marc will go to owners of restaurants and clubs and say something like, "I can bring you fifty beautiful Europeans—some with weird titles— and fifty young, rich, attractive New York socialites, if you'll give ten dollars off on the dinner." So the same group of people will get together every couple of weeks in a new place under fresh circumstances. It's a way of having a nightclub without laying out all the money you need to start a club these days, and of minimizing the risk that people will get bored going to the same place all the time. (Baird Jones created similar events for young preppy Americans in the late Studio 54 period.)

Celebrity Parties

With celebrities, the first time you meet them it blows your mind. But the second time it's just normal; you're already starting to get bored.

It's odd when you know somebody only from the movies and then you meet them in person; and then, of course, you have the opposite thing when you know somebody from the neighborhood and then you see them make it in the movies. Right after I saw Coppola's movie *Cotton Club*, which had Joe Dallesandro, the star of five movies we produced in the Sixties and Seventies, playing Lucky Luciano, somebody asked me which big star I most wanted to meet and I just thought to myself: Joe Dallesandro. I want to meet him *again*.

There's that line of McLuhan's about people not believing that they've been to a concert until they read the review the next day. Well, lots of times you don't know if you've been to a good party until you talk to everybody in the morning and see the columns to find out who actually was there that you couldn't see because you were stuck in a corner and couldn't make it through the crowd to the hot spots.

If it's a celebrity party, the fewer of your own friends who are there, the better, because that means the more people you'll be able to call afterward and make jealous. That's

the game. Some things are less fun to do than they are to say later that you did them. Celebrity parties sometimes fall into this category, because while you're doing it you're thinking who can you tell and how fast after you leave can you find a phone.

Franco Rossellini once described the basic emotion that every person feels when he is: (a) in the company of some fabulous celebrity, (b) getting the royal treatment somewhere, or (c) both. I ran into him at the airport in Rome, where he was just coming in from New York, and with his Italian accent and dramatically blasé delivery, he described the full-blown diplomatic police escort he'd gotten all the way from Manhattan to Kennedy Airport, riding in a limousine sitting between Imelda Marcos and Doris Duke: "The motorcycles are flanking us, the sirens are shrieking, the red lights are flashing, the red carpet is rolling, the traffic is parting, I'm sitting tall in the center, my head is high, Imelda is on my right, Doris is on my left, and"—he clasped his hands together fervently—"in my mind for one thing only I am praying to God, 'Somebody! Please! SEE ME!'"

What the clubs usually do when they're having a party for a celebrity is to have a small, exclusive dinner period at the beginning, at, say,

nine o'clock in the sort of "private" part of the club, not on the main dance floor, and then invite second-level guests in for eleven o'clock, and by midnight or so the private area and the public area have intermixed to a degree—people from the private party are going out to the dance floor, and certain people from the dance floor have talked their way into the private part. Some people just want to be near the celebrity, they crave that proximity, and some of them actually want to talk to them, depending on how pushy they are. At a party like this once at Palladium for Madonna, Beauregard Houston-Montgomery looked around at the by-then homogenized crowd and said, "I think regular people who come to these parties—I mean the ones who *pay* to get in and all that—I think they come expecting something *magic* to happen to them."

I thought about that—People Who Pay looking for Magic. But here's what I think: Celebrities occasionally want to feel real by being with regular people, and regular people want to feel *unreal* by being with celebrities. Celebrities like to keep making sure that they're real, so they go out in the masses to mingle and get a real experience. And then the regular people go looking to get an unreal experience. And these two groups are in

David Belafonte, Duran Duran's Nick Rhodes, and windsurfing champion Jenna de Rosnay

different orbits, always going past each other, in different mental dimensions.

(A technique that party-givers who want to attract celebs sometimes use is giving a party not for a celebrity, but for somebody the celebrities love—like a very popular person in the celebrity community, such as a bodybuilder, a psychic, a drug dealer, a hairdresser, etc. The celebs turn out because they're dependent in some way on this person and want to keep on his good side. And another "subtle" thing the party pros do is invite the less-famous part of a couple or a friendship, knowing this one will bring the famous part.)

I was wondering once how I would feel if I had to go to the same incredibly fabulous celebrity party every night, one with Jack Nicholson and Madonna and Don Johnson and Margaret Thatcher and Billy Martin and Jimmy Swaggart and Lisa Marie Presley and Matt Dillon and Prince—how soon would I get sick of it? It's a tough question, but I think the answer is that on the first night you'd be star-struck and thrilled and everybody would be on good behavior, but then they'd start to get sick of each other, and so each consecutive night their behavior would deteriorate until one night everybody would start to hate everybody else and they'd be pulling out old issues of the *Enquirer* and confronting people with whether they really confided these things to "a friend" about them. So the first night and the last night would be the most fun, for different reasons.

Somebody said to me, "When I meet a celebrity at a party, I'm not just willing to gape in admiration— I want to talk, too. I want to feel that a person who I respect has found *my* conversation interesting." I find this attitude shocking and way out of line. *Celebrities should not be expected to do or say anything at a party.* They *came!* They brought their bodies! Isn't that enough? Great achievers are not necessarily great talkers. I remember a party in a walk-up on 17th Street that I went to in sixty-eight. Jimi Hendrix was

there, a really sweet person, but with his drug problem, he could barely say hello and then he passed out. But so what! The man was *there*, and just by being there—conscious or not—he gave about fifty people the thrill of saying the next day, "I was with Hendrix last night, man." I get annoyed when people are never satisfied. If a celebrity happens to say something witty or be especially nice to you, that's fine, but it's a bonus, totally optional. You shouldn't expect anything. If you do, it's not fair.

Anthropologist Lionel Tiger backs me up on this. He says, "It's quite adequate for a celebrity just to be there. For people who go to a party for a certain celebrity, it's a form of modern, secular pilgrimage—to come into physical contact with the pope of their dreams. That's also why people are willing to pay fifty dollars to see Elizabeth Taylor on stage acting to the best of her ability—they're astonished by the fact that a star is actually right there in front of them. What pilgrimages you make de-

Party-giver Alan Rish and writer Beauregard Houston-Montgomery have different ideas on the question "What do celebrities owe the public?" I saw them having an afternoon breakfast one Sunday at a coffee shop on 9th Street and Second Avenue, and I went in to say hi, then goaded them into reviving their debate.

BHM: I used to be a typical fan, but I've learned that a star can do great work, and that doesn't mean they're not a jerk. I used to think that if you liked somebody's work, they would be wonderful when you met them, but that's not necessarily the case. You have to divorce the two things. That doesn't mean I won't still love a star after I realize he or she's a jerk.

When you go to a party where there's a big celebrity who you love, do you feel disappointed if you don't get a chance to talk to them, or is it enough just that they were there?

BHM: I don't like to talk to my idols—they get on my nerves. I prefer to just see them.

AR: Also, you don't go to a party expecting a celebrity to pay undivided attention to you.

BHM: But the really professional ones do that! They give you their full attention! Diana Ross had a party on that ship the *Intrepid* a few years ago, and there were four hundred people at this party and she spoke to every single one of them. I never saw a human being work a room like that in my life. She worked that battleship. I guess it must have been for her *Swept Away* album. It was a dinner party and all the people there were celebrities except for me—I was the only "non." Dustin Hoffman and all people like that. Michael Musto and I were sort of following her around trying to get a picture of him and her in the same frame without actually bothering her because we were afraid, but suddenly she turned around and said, "Hello, I'm Diana Ross and I'm so happy you came." That's how every star should be—professional and polite.

AR: But you're saying you want them to be undyingly cheerful and charming to everybody. What if a star's personality is not like that? What if their image is not even like that? Why should every celebrity have to be this sweet person? I mean, if you're a bitch, be a bitch. Remember that dinner for Johnny Rotten and he was so rude to us and it was so much fun? And why should a punk star like Wendy O. Williams during her peak be nice to people? Come on! That's ridiculous.

Alan Rish and Beauregard Houston-Montgomery

pend on your values and interests. You may pay to go to a baseball clinic where Pete Rose will come and talk for an hour and chew tobacco. People want the reassurance that celebrities really exist. The whole point in these cases is not to be entertained by them or to talk to them, but to just be in the same room with them."

Circus people, the Unicorn, and John Sex at Area

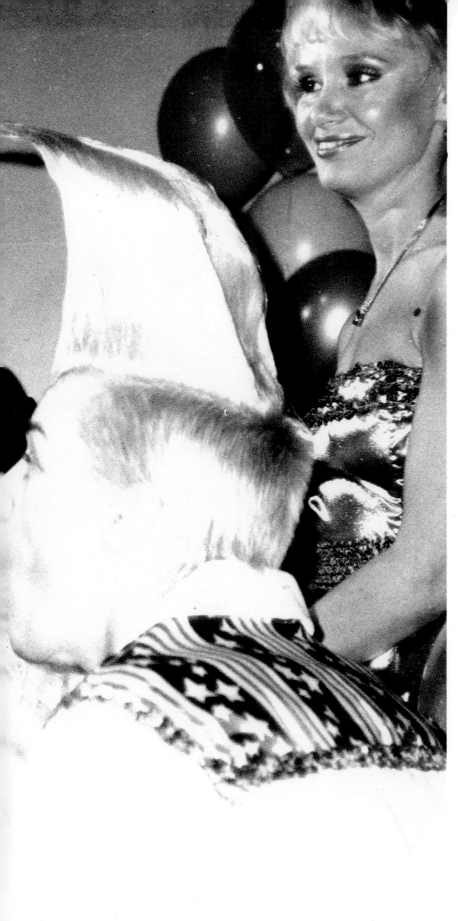

BHM: Punk was a special case. I went to a party for all these great washed-up stars and they were so nice—they introduced themselves and started talking.

AR: They're always nice when they're washed up. I could give fifty parties for one of those old stars and nobody would give a shit.

BHM: But who cares about those Brat Packers? I can't tell one from the other.

AR: Being nice and sweet is fine for the Landers sisters, but who cares about the Landers sisters?

BHM: I love the Landers sisters.

AR: You're just being perverse.

BHM: Professional people should be professional, and if they don't want to be, they should stay home like Garbo. I remember once I was at a party for that movie *Runaway Train,* and everybody was there, from Sheila MacRae to Viva to Matt Dillon. And for the first time, I saw Matt Dillon trying to behave; I think he was influenced by the older people there, so he was making an effort—he actually tried to make conversation.

There is a certain kind of celebrity party where one super-big-at-the-moment star is the draw and, no matter how many other (lesser) celebrities happen to be there, too, "naught is the squire when the king draws high." Here are three examples.

CELEB PARTY #1: THE UNICORN

The difference between human celebrities and animal celebrities is that we have no way of knowing whether an animal wants a career. Or even a job. Probably not. Almost certainly not.

(Here we're talking only about human conditions of celebrity. Certainly a moose, say, wants to be the big celebrity moose in the herd and be feared and respected by all the other males and have sex with all the females he wants; but he's not going to achieve this status by getting a segment on "Entertainment Tonight" or getting the cover of *People* or by giving interviews to magazines about what he's looking for in a mate—a moose will only achieve

The Unicorn arriving by limo

this by winning lots of fights. Magazine covers, etc., are modern *human* conditions of celebrity, and animals don't care about those. And, in fact, if they ever do start to care, too, we'll know we've really hit rock bottom.)

But animals do become celebrities occasionally, for one reason or another, and the people who benefit most from their fame are their owners. The Ringling Brothers, Barnum & Bailey Circus, the owners of "The Living Unicorn," were challenged a couple of years ago by the American Society for the Prevention of Cruelty to Animals to prove that their "unicorn" wasn't just an angora goat with a surgically implanted bull's horn. It made you think of the steroids-for-athletes controversies, and the falsies-and-nose-jobs-in-the-beauty-pageant problems. And you began to wonder what Hollywood would look like if plastic surgery and facelifts were banned. You thought of all the things that people do to their bodies to get their careers moving along. But the unicorn was a special case because if there had been a horn implanted in him, it obviously wasn't because *he* felt he needed it— it was imposed on the poor thing.

So here we had a flesh-and-blood example of a mythical creature who became a reluctant celebrity in the middle of a thirty-three-city tour with the circus. So, to dispel any notion that this "unicorn" wasn't having a great time, the circus decided to have a party for him downtown at Area, with the idea being, I guess, that if the goat liked being a unicorn and a celebrity, he'd *adore* going to a party at a discotheque. And to make sure he had a *really* good time, he'd arrive in a limo. What more could a goat want? It was his first party.

I went down to Area on Hudson Street and met Keith Haring—who had put on a suit and tie for the unicorn—and John Sex, who was having a fight with a circus midget who was hitting him with a rubber hammer and telling him to "get outta the way." I think the circus freaks were jealous of John and his date, Alexis del Lago, who was in drag with an Indian chief's headdress

Director Paul Mazursky with Mike the Dog at a party for *Down and Out in Beverly Hills*

Mr. and Mrs. Jim McMahon with party-giver Carmen D'Alessio

on—they were upstaging the circus people! Eric Goode was helping the circus representatives hand out rose petals to all the people waiting, and a Ringling Brothers representative announced to the crowd that the petals were the unicorn's favorite food. Tiny Lisa Bonet was there waiting, too, but I didn't recognize her until Keith told me because she didn't have makeup on.

Finally the limousine pulled up, they opened the doors, and the goat stepped out, posed for pictures, got showered with rose petals, was led up the steps, placed in a wagon, and wheeled through the long entry hallway of the club into the bar and fountain area. I loved

being next to that goat; it was all fluffed up with something like baby powder. Maybe it was flea stuff. I was petting it and this powder was puffing out, and it felt so soft and like its fur was maybe permanent-waved. He posed for pictures for about ten minutes and then was wheeled out through a back exit door right near the bar, back into, I guess, the limousine, and then taken back to the circus. I asked John Sex why he had turned out for the unicorn and he said, "Well, I always felt a cosmic connection with the symbolism of the unicorn. But what it really comes down to is that I like parties where there's a sure photo opportunity involved."

Chicago Bears-to-be?

A few weeks later the unicorn ran into another problem celebrities face. In fact, it was the very same problem Rosalynn Carter had had once. Remember when that picture of her turned up where she was posing happily with an accused mass murderer? I think it was in Chicago, and when this guy wasn't killing little boys he was active in local politics—that's how he'd met her. Anyway, the *New York Post* ran a story about a man in California who had just committed suicide with a cyanide pill after police began to investigate his connection with the deaths of twenty-five people. With this story the *Post* ran a photograph taken years before, in happier times. It showed a photograph of "The Living Unicorn" taken in pre-stardom days when he went by the name of Lancelot and was living on a ranch in Mendocino County. Beside him in the picture was this man who had just killed himself, and the headline screamed: MASS MURDERER WAS KEEPER OF THE UNICORN.

CELEB PARTY #2: JIM McMAHON

Carmen D'Alessio pulled off a big coup at a peak moment by convincing Jim McMahon—through phone calls to his manager in Chicago—to let the Palladium throw a party for him. This was moments after the Bears won the Super Bowl,

Fred Dryer

while the Super Bowl Shuffle video was still playing on MTV, and during the week he happened to be on the cover of *Rolling Stone*. Snaring the hot person at the hot moment—the dream of every professional party-giver.

Because of the exposure he had in the music video, I guess, even people who weren't into sports knew who he was—that he was this cute football player who always wore a headband and sunglasses. (He had such large cross-culture appeal that this party for him wound up outgrossing the one they'd had for Madonna in the middle of her *Like a Virgin* tour.) The idea of the Palladium full of athletes for a change, instead of the usual clubsters, was appealing. The invitation said the party started early, at nine or something, so we went to Mr. Chow's first for dinner, where we were meeting Nick Rhodes from Duran Duran and his wife, Juliana, and some other people I'd never met before, including Alan Freed's grandson Robert and Harry Belafonte's son David, who said he was a diehard football fan. So we ate fast in case athletes were more prompt at parties than rock-and-rollers, and then got cabs down to the Palladium.

Your hair's very Joey Heatherton, Nick. Did you do it up especially for the party?

I didn't even know we were going to a party.

So you're *semper paratus* for a party?

Oh, semper, yes.

How are you going to compete with the football players who'll be there?

I'm in competition only by contrast. I have no muscles whatsoever. Only the ones I can sculpt in with makeup. And I have better shoulder pads in my white silk moiré coat than they'll ever have. They're the ones who'll have to compete because they haven't got white moiré coats—yet.

When we got to the Palladium, naturally they weren't there yet—Carmen usually says nine and it

Anthony Haden-Guest

means three A.M.—so we went up to the Mike Todd Room and checked out the crowd. Captain Kevin, one of the DJs from radio station Z-100, pointed out New York Giants Karl Banks, William Roberts, and Leonard Marshall, plus a few New York Knicks and Seattle Supersonics, who had been playing the Knicks that night. But I wasn't close enough to get pictures. David Belafonte said it was hard to recognize football players in street clothes, and he was right. Then suddenly at eleven o'clock the word came that they had arrived at the front door, so everyone got excited, and in a few minutes Carmen and Steve Rubell appeared at one end of the Mike Todd Room with Jim McMahon and his wife and began to take the room yard by yard with everybody mobbing him. Nikki Haskell screamed, "He's gorgeous!" and a girl next to her said, "But isn't he married and like a Mormon or something?" And Nikki said, "Like a Mormon/Like a Virgin—who cares? He's gorgeous!"

This trip through the room was for one purpose only: to let everybody see McMahon once, to let them know that they had been not just at a party *for* him but *with* him.

Athletes are so heroic that, even more than movie stars, their mere presence is enough for the crowd: They're not chosen as guests of honor because of their articulateness or their lively personalities—just for things like their hand-eye coordination.

So McMahon made his way in a straight line from one end of the room to the other—just enough to let people feel he had walked among them—and then everybody was happy. In a situation like this, you don't expect someone to stay on and socialize. After that, he and his wife and a few other people went into one of the private rooms and spent the rest of the party there.

This type of celebrity party falls into the unicorn category because it just means one straight tour by the celebrity through the party room and then out the door, and everybody is happy, that's all they needed. You were there and so was he.

Comedian Joey Adams and columnist Cindy Adams

Professional photographer Quinto

Michael Jackson and publicist Susan Blond

CELEB PARTY #3: MICHAEL JACKSON

The Michael Jackson party, however, wasn't as complete as the Unicorn and McMahon parties, because Michael never made that one, essential, obligatory celebrity push through the crowd. But there were extenuating circumstances—Michael had caught on fire while filming a Pepsi commercial the week before the party. Susan Blond, the engineer of the party, explains:

The Michael Jackson party at the Museum of Natural History was I guess the greatest party I ever organized because it'll go down in history. Not natural history, maybe, but media history. At that moment he was the most popular person in the whole world; he'd just gone in the *Guinness Book of Records* for being the number-one record seller in the world. Right after this he went on the *Victory* tour and then there was a certain backlash, but before the tour, his appeal was total. To throw a party that huge, I called the two people who know the most about huge parties and crowd control—Steve Rubell and Ian Schrager. They were in-between clubs—Studio 54 and the Palladium—which means it was in that period when they had just gotten out of jail and were in the halfway house, so they had time to help while they were gearing up for their nightlife comeback. They were connected to people in the city government, so they could call somebody who could call somebody who could get us the right amount of police. A lot of people helped me—people who had worked with Paul McCartney had faced a lot of these crowd problems, but this was going to be bigger than anything.

The invitation in the shape of one glove was my brilliant idea. Today it's a collector's item. And although it was the four presidents of CBS Records who were on the invitation as hosts, I was determined my name would be on it someplace, so I put "RSVP Susan Blond" at the bottom. Just like a secetary, but still it was *there*.

For every party I try to get as much for free as possible, but when they would hear the name Michael Jackson, they saw dollar signs, so it

was impossible. We had to pay whatever it cost us, plus pay the museum union people for the privilege of not using them. Every time our people turned on a switch, we had to pay them as if *they* had turned on a switch. It cost a fortune. And you know all those people who were just indicted in the scandals at City Hall? They all wanted to come—borough presidents and things.

You should have seen us leave the hotel that night with Michael and Brooke Shields and the brothers and the rest of the family. Instead of geting a police escort, Rubell got in one of the limos up front and he would run out into the street and direct the traffic in his tuxedo and people would just do whatever he said! He had mapped out an exact route and we'd done a few run-throughs about how we were going to get there and get Michael into the right secret room. That was a big criticism of the party—that Michael was in the secret room the whole time. People were screaming at me, "Shouldn't we be able to *see* this man? This isn't a Roman victory celebration, you know!" But you have to consider, Michael had been on fire the week before the party. Remember? That Pepsi commercial? The first night after the fire we only cared about Michael, whether he was okay or not, but the second day we started asking, "Will he make it to the party?"

The number of celebrities who came was not overwhelming. Julian Lennon was there, and Mary Tyler Moore, but they didn't come out for it like they would've if we'd given a small party at "21" or someplace where they would've felt certain they'd meet him.

Michael did go out to wave to the crowd a few times, because they were standing in that below-ten-degree weather.

We had made up a ten-thousand-dollar globe that showed he was platinum all over the world. It lit up and it had a four-foot radius—you needed something big and spinning to show up in a place as big as the museum. Unfortunely it broke on the way there and we eventually had another one built for another ten thousand, but it was well worth

it, because Michael saves everything and he put it in his own private museum.

Then we paid dancers to do somersaults and things before Michael got there, but he arrived ahead of schedule, so they were somersaulting all around him and he didn't know where to stand, how to get out of their way.

Then there was a big burst of confetti, like a night at Studio 54 would've had, and that was the real climax moment. We have all this on tape if you ever want to see it. February 7, 1984.

CELEBRITY PHOTOGRAPHER

Most people know Ron Galella as the photographer Jackie O took to court for photographing her at close range. I've been seeing Ron all over town for years—he's always the most conspicuous photographer covering any party because physically he's big and he's also the most aggressive, which I like: He's focused and he pushes for what he wants.

I phoned to interview Ron about his work. He lives up in Westchester, and while someone went out to the yard to get him, I talked to his wife, Betty. They met while she was a vice president of Today Is Sunday, *a glossy Sunday supplement magazine in Washington, D.C., and now together they run his free-lance photography business. I asked Betty if Ron has lots of people who tip him off as to when celebrities are going to be someplace. She told me, "He generally just relies on twenty-five years of experience. Celebrities, especially, are creatures of habit. They stay at the same hotels, they eat in the same restaurants, they shop in the same stores—they don't change their routines much." I wondered how Ron chooses which events to go to, and if there are ways to know immediately if an event will be good or not. "You know the social engagements column and the 'Follow Up on the News' in the* New York Times *on Sunday?" she said. "Well, any event that's listed for a social charity function that has a ticket price under three hundred dollars Ron won't cover. Because the price alone brings out the riffraff."*

By this time Ron had picked up the phone. He heard what Betty said and began our interview by qualifying it:

No, let me say that even more

than the price of the tickets, the big question is "Who?" That's what you always have to ask yourself, because this is a "who" business—who's going to be there? The tickets may be cheap, but a big celebrity may have a soft spot for that cause. So "Who?" is more important than "How much?"

Where did you go last night?

First I went to the Waldorf for the tribute to Arthur and Mathilde Krim. She's a doctor. I'm surprised they got all the celebrities they did.

I think he was in the movie business.

Ah, that would explain it. Senator Kennedy was there and Vice President Mondale, and Robert Strauss was master of ceremonies. Warren Beatty came. And Woody Allen with Mia Farrow—just for an hour, but that was fair enough. He gave of himself. I got some good pictures; I just finished printing them up. Warren Beatty shook my hand—he knows me very well. I followed him and Julie Christie around the world for a year when they were having their affair. Once in Geneva he turned around and said, "How the hell do you get around?" I said, "I use the same planes you do."

How long did you stay at the Waldorf thing?

I left that superstar party long before anybody else did for a couple of very good reasons. First, I overheard a photographer from the *Post* say that he wasn't going to bother going over to the party called Broadway Salutes Lincoln Center, so I realized that like him, a lot of the press was probably going to skip it and therefore if I went, I would be getting exclusive fashion shots of the regular stars who would be going there. Not superstars, just regular stars—Bea Arthur, Stockard Channing, Shirley Jones, Madeline Kahn, Mark Hamill, Leslie Uggams, Dick Shawn. Second, I'd gotten pictures of everybody at the Waldorf already, and although the Kennedy kids—Jackie's kids—were coming, I'm not allowed to photograph them. So I

Ron Galella

went across town, and the lesser event at Lincoln Center did turn out to be more valuable to me than the big one because I was the only photographer there, and a lot of the stars had beautiful and colorful gowns on—fashion shots that I can sell to the tabloids and *People.* Lillian Montevecchi had a very sexy outfit on that showed her legs, and the PR people there like me and invited me in to the party. So I milked the event. It was a good decision.

Have you always worked free-lance?

Yeah. But the whole field is changed now from when I started. In the old days, a romance like Warren and Julie's sold all over, there were so many movie and TV magazines—about thirty of them—*Photoplay, Modern Screen, Motion Picture*—so many. And they were all very hungry for gossip pictures, new romances. That's what made me go into this business. And that's why I selected Jackie for fifty percent of my business. In 1970 I only got about twenty good takes of Jackie, and yet that was one of my best years, because there was a tremendous market. It was easy for me to get pictures of Jackie because we both lived in New York. All I had to do was "get up and go to work"—follow her from her apartment to the ballet to the theater to the restaurant, etc. This is why I did it—because it was convenient.

But I thought you were still allowed to photograph her, but only from twenty-five feet.

No, not anymore. The first court battle they said I could photograph Jackie from twenty-five feet and the kids from thirty. But then the second case I lost.

You must have been dying for your camera.

Right, it was frustrating to sit there in court without it. They figured I broke the twenty-five-feet injunction four times. The truth was—and I told them this—I'd broken it hundreds of times and Jackie didn't seem to care. The only reason she brought me to court again is that she was influenced to do it, I feel. She was with Maurice

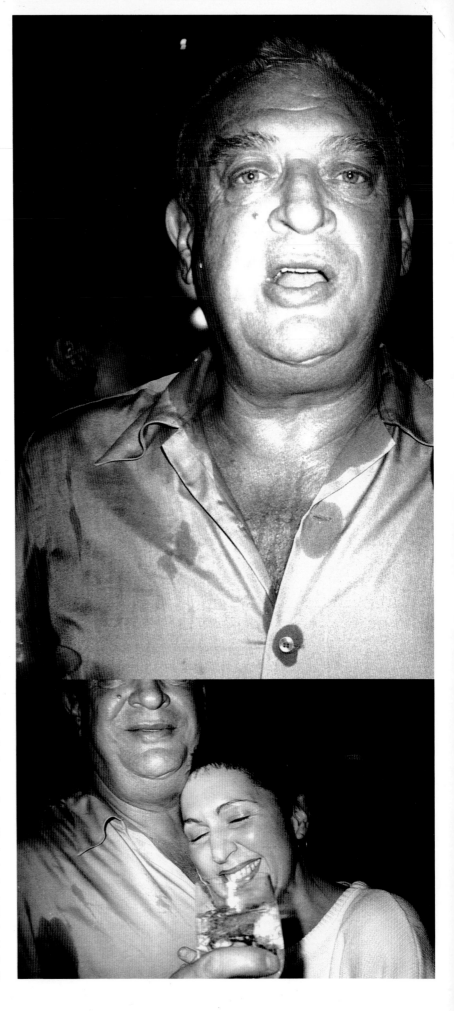

Rodney Dangerfield at a press party for his movie *Back to School*. (below left) A fan has pushed her way past the *Entertainment Tonight* crew, thrown herself into Rodney's arms, and muttered quickly that she "needs" a picture. A friend standing by with a instant-focus camera gets the shot. (below) A more "posed" situation.

Actress Sylvia Miles

Tempelsman and I shot them when they were coming out of the Winter Garden Theater from *Cats,* and he took her right to the police station to press charges. It's impractical to shoot from twenty-five feet back. Look how many people could be in front of me, heads popping up, obstructing the view. The judge did everything he could to me. I had a very good lawyer, Marvin Mitchelson, and he talked to the judge, who wanted to give me seven years in jail and a one-hundred-twenty-five-thousand-dollar fine. Both! They talked, trying to figure what I could give up. Well, the only thing I had was Jackie and the kids,

so the judge made it a ten-thousand-dollar fine plus giving that up. Mind you, her lawyer was agreeing to five thousand and the judge said, "No, that's too little—make it ten thousand." That's the kind of judge I had. Anyway, if I had taken a photograph of Caroline or John at the Waldorf last night, I could've gotten a hundred-twenty-five-thousand-dollar fine and seven years in jail. To stay out of jail I had to give up Jackie and the kids forever.

It's sad. You were like the family photographer.

Yeah, it's sad, and it goes even

further—I can't hire my wife or anybody else to photograph them. I hope this will change. My lawyer says that once the judge passes away—he's eighty-six—things could get better.

People have so many affairs right out in public now, and they admit so much, there aren't too many "scandals" anymore. What's the hottest celebrity picture you can imagine?

There don't seem to be as many big hot pictures around, because the trend is to more celebrities, so each one isn't so big. Like with the Brat Pack, Molly Ringwald's the best of them. I have to work a lot harder today—take a lot of pictures of a lot of different stars. The prices magazines pay for pictures hasn't gone up over the years, and yet the cost of labor and materials has sky-rocketed. Paper has gone up five to ten percent every year. *People* and *Us*, they request people who aren't really superstars, so you have to keep files on them. Estée Lauder is an example. Or the chicken guy, Perdue. You wouldn't believe who they ask for. They even want Mickey Mouse and Donald Duck—it's unbelievable. Sometimes they want you to get pictures of romances that don't exist, which is impossible. I have to sell dozens of pictures of Betsy Bloomingdale to equal that one great picture of Liz and Dick. And when a star comes alone to a party, it's not a major event. Like if Warren last night had come with Isabelle Adjani or something, that would've been a *biiiig* picture.

What do magazines pay for pictures?

About what they paid years ago, still. Just fifty to a hundred dollars for a black-and-white. *People* will pay maybe a hundred. The *Enquirer* pays better, maybe two fifty for a black-and-white.

How do you always know what's going on?

I watch the papers and I subscribe to Earl Blackwell's *Bulletin*, which is another thing that just went up. It costs about a thousand dollars a year, but it's very reliable. Sometimes you don't need information, you just hit it right. I live in Yonkers, so sometimes on my way home I'll stop at Elaine's just to check it. Sometimes I get lucky there.

How do you get along with PR people?

Some of them can be so stupid. I'll give you an example. Remember that movie *The Greek Tycoon* that was all about Jackie and Onassis, but with the names changed? Well, they were shooting it in Regine's and the PR people were letting all these other photographers in and were keeping me out!

They were acting like they had the real Jackie in there.

Yeah! And if they weren't so stupid, they would've realized that it would've made their movie much more real to have me in it, to show that I'm the one who goes after Jackie. That's how much imagination they have. Some PR people try to control too much. Whereas the stars themselves kind of like me, to tell you the truth. Except Jackie, maybe. But even Brando—after knocking my teeth out, he's nice to me. I think he learned a lesson from that incident—it cost him twenty thousand dollars. Stars recognize me, which is my big edge. I have Jackie to thank for this—those court battles made me so infamous that I get great shots from their reactions.

When do stars get annoyed?

When you overshoot. But I could shoot Joan Collins a hundred times and she loves it. It depends on the person.

Who are your favorite stars?

There's so many, really. Dustin Hoffman, Warren Beatty, Woody Allen—Isabella Rossellini is one of my favorites, like Ingrid Bergman was. And Liz Taylor—we've both been around so long, we're like survivors. I'm surviving in paparazzi and she's surviving in her career. *(laughs)* And in love.

When's the best time to shoot people?

I like to get people leaving restaurants, because when they're going in they're hungry and in a rush to eat, but coming out they're wined and dined and they stop and pose. At parties it could go either way; you never know if you'll get better pictures when they're arriving or departing. There are some celebrities that you get to know show up late. Cher is always late. You allow for these habitual latecomers.

How do they pick which photographers to let in to an event and which ones stay outside?

Sometimes PR people won't let you in because you didn't call and get on the list. Petty, petty, petty. So you have to shoot outside on the street. But getting in doesn't always mean you get the best. When *Scarface* premiered, the party was at Sardi's. I was not on the list, so I had to stay outside on the street while every other photographer was inside. I waited and finally Al Pacino came out with his girlfriend Kathleen Quinlan. I got a great shot of them—him looking at me with his eyes popping—getting into his car. Luckily the car glass was clear so I was able to shoot through it. Now, I was the only one who got a picture of them together, because inside he was only posing with the cast. Mine was the best. So, when stars pose they're usually not at their best. Inside was posed, but coming out was private, and that's what I got. I do pretty good outside. I don't give up when I don't get in.

"THE ENVELOPE, PLEASE"

Remembering all those starlets out in California who used to make publicity appearances at the openings of supermarkets, during the Seventies the press began to say that party-loving Academy Award–winning actress Sylvia Miles "would go to the opening of an envelope." Sylvia retorts:

"I highly resent being known as the person who'd go to the opening of an envolope. That image has done damage to my career. And the ironic thing is, it started because a journalist asked me if I'd gone to a certain opening, and I laughed and replied, 'Listen, if I'd gone to that, I'd go to the opening of an envelope.' The press picked up on that and began using my own line against me! When I was doing *Vieux Carré* in England and was gone from New York for a whole year, friends sent me clippings from the newspapers that had me at this party and that party, calling me the 'omnipresent Sylvia Miles,' and I wasn't even in this country! You see, when press agents send you an invitation, sometimes they tell the columnists, 'Invited are . . .' and then they print that list and don't check back to see if you really went. It takes a long time to live down a one-liner."

Ann Turkel, producer Doug Cramer, and Alana Stewart

Gavin MacLeod and Joan Collins

Out-of-Town Parties

HOLLYWOOD PARTIES

The timing was perfect on a trip I made out to L.A. a couple of years ago when I was asked to be on *The Love Boat.* I'd read the script, seen that it was only about three lines, and knew I'd be able to handle that—nothing strenuous like *Miami Vice.* The week of filming would coincide not only with the Oscars, meaning that I could go to Swifty and Mary Lazar's big Academy Awards party at the restaurant Spago, but also to the huge party Doug Cramer and Aaron Spelling were giving for the thousandth guest star on *Love Boat.* The identity of the thousandth was being kept a mystery until the party—I was the nine hundred ninety-ninth.

The Lazar party was so great and the praise for it was getting so wild that Swifty finally had to protest, "Look, I'm not an institution—I'm just giving a *party!*"

It was hard to watch the actual Academy Awards show on TV in the restaurant. I like to really study everything because there's only one thing we *really* watch the Oscars

Irving "Swifty" Lazar on Oscar night

105

DOUGLAS S. CRAMER PRODUCTIONS IN ASSOCIATION WITH AARON SPELLING PRODUCTIONS
EXECUTIVE PRODUCERS: AARON SPELLING AND DOUGLAS S. CRAMER
WARNER HOLLYWOOD STUDIOS • 1041 NORTH FORMOSA AVENUE, LOS ANGELES, CALIFORNIA 90046 • PHONE (213) 850-2500

October 4th, 1985

Mr. Andy Warhol
c/o Vincent Freemont
Andy Warhol Studios
19 East 32nd Street
New York, N.Y. 10016

Dear Mr. Warhol:

I am pleased to inform you that your LOVE BOAT episode
will air on Saturday, October 12th, at 10:00pm, on ABC.

Enjoy!!!

Best regards,

Elaine Strom

Elaine Strom
Assistant to

Dennis Hammer
Producer

for—that's to see which stars have been doing the most nipping and tucking and lifting and transplanting and spa-going (as opposed to Spago-ing). Usually I like to watch in a group where people are assigned different areas to scrutinize—there are nose-job squads, rug patrols—a division of labor, everyone looking out for their specialties, sharing their expertise with the group as a whole. Twentieth Century-Fox vice president Susan Pile has the practical Joan Crawford approach: She covers her four TVs with clear plastic wrap, then hands out water pistols, and everyone vents their opinions of the stars' speeches and outfits that way. But watching the show on the monitors. At Spago, everyone was on better behavior than that. And then, of course, after the real event was finished downtown, all the rest of the stars filed in. It's odd being right there in L.A. for the Awards, though, because it starts when it's still light out. I just couldn't get

Cary Grant

Gavin MacLeod

used to that. *Interview* editor Gael Love was there with *Hollywood Reporter* and *Interview* columnist George Christy, and I pulled George into a corner and asked him to tell me, since he knew Hollywood so well, how he decided which parties to go to. He told me:

"After a while you do get a radar about what might be good copy. From my point of view, there are two kinds of parties—the ones you go to for pictures, because they'll be colorful and glamorous, and the ones where you might get some good information. You balance it, and sometimes you have to go to several to get what you need. If I think I might have a party photographed, I need to see a guest list beforehand to see whether it's worth it or not to have the photographer there. Because you're dealing with cash here; the photographer is paid by the assignment— they're not on staff, you see. I have to make sure it's a worthy job for the publication to spend money on. With private parties, of course, you don't photograph.

"If I go to a party and realize that it's not right for me, I stay politely and then I manage to duck out. Occasionally you'll go to a party where people are, well, you know, nice, but it isn't really working for you, it's a snore. This doesn't happen very often because my radar's pretty good, but once or twice a year I'll

Milton Berle

make a mistake, and then I'll say, 'I have to make a phone call.' And I will go check my service or something and slip out the door. Listen, you have to."

I asked George if, when he gave parties, he had trouble with celebrities who said they were coming and then didn't show up. He said, "Never mind when they're supposed to show up and they don't—what about when they RSVP no and then they *do* come? And it's a seated dinner? But when you're dealing with actors, a lot of times it's not their fault when they cancel at the last minute. Catherine Oxenberg, for example, was coming to a dinner and at the last minute she called and said that there was a very slow director doing that particular segment of *Dynasty*, so she didn't know how long she'd be. You see? But of course, when they arrive you just have to be very cool and redo everything, because after all, how wonderful to have them there!"

That afternoon when I was riding down Sunset back from the *Love Boat* set, the driver had looked at a tall new structure and called it a "see-through building," meaning that they were having trouble renting it. And being crowded together at Spago, I realized, was fun—so much better than a "see-through party," where the space is too large for the number of people. It's always better to be squeezed at a party than not squeezed—it gets things going. People love to be tight, that's what they're there for—they can get elbow room at home.

In New York you can move from party to party in mobs—it's like a big blob moving around the city from party to party, from club to club. But in L.A. it's very under control; people just get into cars and ride long distances for an event. It's not like in New York: "If we don't like this one, we'll just go around the corner . . ."

The *Love Boat* party was everything I'd hoped it would be—every star from Joan Collins to Fred Travalena, from Englebert Humperdinck to Joanne Worley. Roddy McDowall and Troy Donahue were at our table. Ginger Rogers and Mary Martin were across from us.

Caesar Romero and Jane Wyatt were at the next table. Gavin MacLeod did some comedy routines and the Mermaid Dancers came out strutting and swaying. All during that week I'd worked with my co–guest stars Marion Ross, Raymond St. Jacques, Andy Griffith, Milton Berle, and Peter Duchin—and, of course, with all the regulars on the crew, who were all great. So I had been gradually acclimated to seeing great stars, but really, the mix was even greater than some of its parts—like Dina Merrill and Alexis Smith and Red Buttons. It was all just great, a thrill a minute. Lots of favorites you were worried might be dead by then, but there they were, still looking great. However, the shockeroo came when they started a salute to everyone who had died after appearing on *The Love Boat*, when they started showing clips from each dead person's appearance on the show. You just couldn't believe how many there were. It was like you were seeing the Curse of the Love Boat—Richard Basehart, Joan Blondell, James Broderick, Judy Canova, Jan Clayton, Hans Conried, Bob Crane, Richard Deacon, Janet Gaynor, Will Geer, Arthur Godfrey, Joan Hackett, Patsy Kelly, Fernando Lamas, Peter Lawford, Ethel Merman, Slim Pickens, Walter Slezak . . . just on and on. It seemed like forever, although it probably wasn't more than thirty—which isn't too bad out of a thousand guest stars—but just seeing them all together, people who you'd forgotten had died, even, had its impact. It got me wondering how much more time I had left. After that they seemed to be stalling when they started showing "highlights" from past episodes. (I could hear someone whispering, "These are the *high*lights? The *high*lights?!") And finally, the big moment arrived and they brought out the surprise thousandth guest passenger on the Boat—Lana Turner. I think Lana had been late arriving or something. And then my name was called to go up on stage and join a line of stars surrounding Doug Cramer and Aaron Spelling. Great party—balloons, favors, dancing, the works. And then it was

over and we left the Beverly Hilton and went out to wait for our car.

People who park cars in L.A. are trained, I think, to be just as discriminating as the doormen at New York clubs, because I notice they park the cars in descending order of importance. The Rollses are all in the front. It's all valet parking out there, of course, and the cars are calibrated by these valets, so the quicker you get to get out of a place determines how important you are, based on the status of your car.

Sometimes invitations in L.A. are

Dina Merrill

odd, so that even if you think you're invited, you're not really all that invited. The great old etiquette books have beautiful, flowery invitations like, "Bill and I would place it high among our summer's pleasures if you and Jane could come out next weekend . . ." Contrast that with this: Keith Haring was talking about some art things with Cher, and she gave him two phone numbers and said for him to call her the next day. Keith and I were both staying at the same hotel; we were having lunch by the pool. Keith went away to call Cher and when he came

back, he said that a recording had come on and said, "We're staying home this afternoon having a barbecue, and if you have this number it's probably okay to just drop in." We'd been looking for something to do, so that sounded good, but we didn't know Cher's address. However, Cher's house happened to be on the market, and someone who was with us happened to have just been to look at it, so she gave us the address. We went out to Cher's place, rang the buzzer, and said, "It's Andy Warhol and Keith Haring." And they said, "Oh, uh, gee, well, uh, okay, I guess." And they let us in, but they really were shocked. Apparently she'd forgotten she'd given Keith that number. But after a while they got used to having us there and it was fun. Keith played with Cher's kid, Elijah Blue, and with Geraldo Rivera's son. And there was a copy of that week's *National Star* around—it had Cher on the cover—and everybody one by one read the article, but nobody wanted to be the one to ask her if the stuff was true or not.

And here's another Hollywood invitation. This one happened to Whitney Tower Jr., a socialite who now works in public relations at L'Agence. A few years ago Whitney was out in L.A. looking for acting jobs. He told me, "I met Allan Carr at a party one night and he invited me to his house for a seven-thirty 'breakfast meeting' the next morning. He was producing all these movies that had lots of parts for guys my age in them and I could hardly sleep, I was so excited. At six-thirty A.M. my phone rang and it was some sort of houseboy. He said, 'Mr. Tower?' and I said, 'Yes.' he said, 'I understand you have a meeting set for this morning with Mr. Carr?' I sad, 'Yes! Yes! I'll be there!' And he said, 'Tell me, did Mr. Carr invite you for "full" or "continental?"' I said, 'Gee, I don't know—I'll eat anything.' And when I hung up the phone it sank in that that established my importance—how long my meeting was set for, whether I would be given time to eat a doughnut or blueberry pancakes with hot chocolate. It turned out I got a croissant."

Rupert Everett and photographer Paul Jasmin

Cher

Tony Danza

JOHN KOBAL AND DONALD LYONS— PARTIES IN MOVIES

John Kobal is a film historian who's written books on Garbo, Monroe, and Hayworth, and his personal collection of Hollywood film stills is legendary. Donald Lyons is a teacher and film critic.

Are parties in movies mainly women's territory?

JK: John Wayne would go to parties, but probably just to pick up his wife. He'd go off with his buddies in the kitchen and they'd all play cards.

DL: Clint Eastwood would only be at a party to investigate somebody. He'd walk through looking for a suspect. A couple of women would "ooh" and "ah" in the distance and he'd dismiss them the way he dismisses them. Then he'd go after the dope dealer and break some window with a view of the Pacific Ocean.

Even if Clark Gable was at a party, it wouldn't be in his head—parties don't matter to him. Jeff Bridges would be nice at a party—he'd stay late and help you clean up.

JK: Except for Cary Grant, men aren't party girls. You see him at parties the way you would see a woman. I'm not saying he's a sissy, but the other men at parties are like Clifton Webb, who looks like he's spent his life in front of a pencil sharpener. Cary Grant is the ideal single male you could get for a party when you're missing a man. What you would really wind up with would be Franklin Pangborne, who I can only see living in a teacup.

Who are the big party girls?

JK: Ava Gardner was a great party girl, but she actually was mostly in nightclubs. When you look like Ava and you have her grace, people *rememmmber* you. And Rita Hayworth, too. They were both nightclub girls. Their role in life is circumscribed, but they had innate decency and a good sense of humor. They didn't feel put down because men liked to show them off— they just thought, Well why not? What was their alternative? When you're as beautiful as those two, you're always going to attract a crowd, and you look for places where this won't be an obstruction to your own fun, so you spend a lot of time in smoky nightclubs. . . . Marlene Dietrich was a great party girl, but you hardly ever see her at parties in movies. I can only think of *Dishonored*, where she comes as a knight in a short skirt and the boots and the helmet. You see, Dietrich *used* parties, and therefore they weren't really parties. She's one of those people who in a crowd of two thousand knows exactly what she's looking for, finds it, then leaves. Oh, she'll blow on the streamers, she'll turn and laugh, but the glass will never spill. Immaculate. The party isn't what it's about for her. And later on when she was a down-to-earth girl with Von Sternberg, if she were a madame in a brothel giving a party, she'd make damn sure everybody was having a good time, and she'd *look* like *she* was having one, but you would know that deep down it was strictly something she would lay on. She's not *involved* in the party. . . . Marilyn Monroe was a walking party—you could even imagine her carrying the groceries home for the party. And the way she'd walk down the street, you'd know she was going to a party later that evening. . . . If Tallulah were giving a party, all you'd think is, "I hope she doesn't notice me." You'd want to be there, and you'd know it was going to be an incredible pitch, but you'd just pray she wouldn't pick on you. She intoxicated people. I think she even gave them hangovers. . . . Bette Midler's a great party girl. I'd love to be at a party with her—she reminds me of all the Joan Blondells, the Ann Southerns. . . . A party with Bette Davis is something anybody could use in their memoirs. Davis is the best party-giver and -goer. Think of when Davis walks into the cotillion in *Jezebel*—was it the cotillion?— wearing a red dress when everyone who hasn't been raped or disfigured by sex is supposed to be wearing white. She's paid no attention to everyone who's told her not to do it, and she walks in with her mortified escort, Henry Fonda. She takes off her cape and—now it's too late! It's that classic situation where you dream that you're naked and you hope nobody sees you. But Davis pays her dues, and that's what makes the fun even better. You don't have to avert your eyes when you see her the next day—*she* won't be embarrassed, she's too strong. She's contemporary. And the exact same thing could be said for Vivien Leigh: Those two aren't rattled by society—society's rattled by them. *Gone With the Wind* is a wonderful party movie. Right at the beginning Scarlett's tired of war talk and says, "Waw-uh, waw-uh, waw-uh! If I hea-uh one more wuhd about waw-uh, ah-m not goin' ta tha bahbecue!"

DL: She's the spirit of Party—bitchy self-aggrandizement—and it's very refreshing. She'll do anything if it's contrary. At the ball where the widows are raising money for the war and Scarlett's just lost her husband, you know she doesn't really care. There's a raffle and the person who bids the highest can ask the young ladies to dance, and so Rhett is going to ask Scarlett, who at first is going to pretend that she's as outraged as any old biddy there that he's asking her while she's "in mourning." But when she sees all the outrage on the faces of those biddies, irritating them becomes more important to her than turning Rhett down! So she quickly calculates who's going to be the most upset and acts accordingly and dances with Rhett. She's fun, she's fun.

The Sixties movies had great party scenes.

DL: I have two favorites from that period. First is *Beyond the Valley of the Dolls*. This homicidal maniac drag queen called Z-man gives a drug freak-out party with his big blond boyfriend in a Malibu mansion and there's two great lines in it. Somebody says, "What time does the party start?" and they're told, "What time does any party start? When you get there." And then there's an all-girl group in the movie—they're the Carrie Nations—and one of them turns to the others and says, "I've been at parties where they played Straw-

Molly Ringwald

Joan Quinn and Larry Hagman

Demi Moore

berry Alarm Clock records, but this is the first party I've been to where Strawberry Alarm Clock actually played." And then in the great Roger Corman motorcycle movie *Wild Angels,* one of the bikers has been killed—probably Bruce Dern and probably by the cops—and the Angels have taken over this town and have the funeral in this white clapboard church. The body is on the altar and the widowed biker mama approaches—a wonderful actress named Joan Sawlee—in a black dress and a black veil. She goes up the wooden steps, opens the church doors, sees that the bikers are screwing and drinking, having an orgy on the altar, throws back her veil and screams, "It's PARTY TIME!" . . . *The Big Chill* is about nostalgia for parties, really—about the notion that the Sixties were a party and that we miss it all now. So they have a kooky little version of it—a suburban re-creation of Youth as Party.

What about the Brat Pack movies?

DL: The party in *St. Elmo's Fire* is probably the best of the Brat Pack parties. If you went to college, and you went to graduate school, you probably went through a phase like that and it captures being in one's early twenties very well. It's not a glamorization of the creepiness. One of them has a job working for a bizarre Korean millionaire in Washington, D.C., and they take over the house—this plot is not worth going into—but it captures the feeling of kids having a party in a big place they don't belong in.

What about not getting invited to parties?

JK: Audrey Hepburn didn't go to more parties in her movies than probably anybody else. She looked in at them from the outside—from the chauffeur's house: "Oh, the men in tuxedos! All the women are so beautiful!" She doesn't have an evil bone in her body. It doesn't even enter her mind that any of them would be saying anything that isn't funny or charming or stylish. She's the girl outside, but as she looks in, the more you think, "This

girl is where the party is really taking place."

One of my favorite parties is in *A Place in the Sun*, when Liz Taylor takes Montgomery Clift in her arms—the way she looked then, she was everything that you ever think when you're outside will be waiting for you if only you could get in. When Liz takes him in, he's "in." His clothes lose their creases, everything about him suddenly becomes right, he doesn't have to try anymore.

JK: The two of them *live* in a close-up, don't they? "Come to Mama," she says, and that's IT.

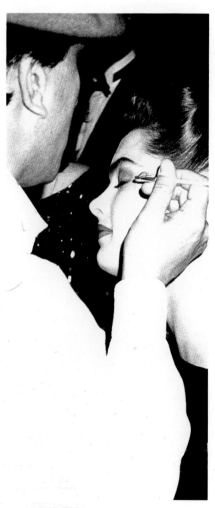

Brooke Shields

And Cecil B. De Mille gave great imitation parties. You could see that the grapes were plastic, but it didn't matter. They looked like orgies, they sounded like orgies, and people talked as if they were at an orgy—the only difference is you didn't see any sex.

JK: Greece was all about keeping

your toga clean, and Rome was about getting it stained.

DL: But parties are only interesting when they're not fun—when they're places of suffering. The greatest movie party of all is in Visconti's *The Leopard.* At the end there's a ball given for the whole Sicilian aristocracy. At this party Burt Lancaster, the prince, the hero, comes to terms with the existence of the younger generation, who he doesn't particularly understand or even like—his crassly ambitious nephew, Alain Delon, and the beautiful middle-class girl, Claudia Cardinale. He dances with her in a very beautiful sequence, and seeing the rhythms of this party, he accepts his own death. And it's the closest thing to a tragic party that the movies have ever done. The girls are all jumping around and hundreds of young people are making noise, and he says, "With the next evolutionary turn, they'll all be hanging from trees by their tails again." The character leaves this party as if he were leaving parties forever, and in fact he goes out and dies. The best parties are about intense alienation and solitude—like the one in *Sunset Boulevard.* Gloria Swanson tells William Holden that she's going to take him to an incredible New Year's Eve party in the very house where Valentino died and in the very pool where Pola Negri swam, etc. She deceives him into thinking that all of Old Hollywood is going to be there. And it turns out she's had her own mansion decorated and hired eighty blindfolded musicians and invited nobody but *him.* She's made the party a kind of sex trap. Party as Prison. Party as Deception. A magnificently glamorous party, but it's just for two. Then he leaves there to go to a party with his co-evals at Jack Webb's house, and this party is full of noisy good will and unbuttoned fun, but it's much less interesting than the insanity of the party at Swanson's mansion. Here you have a "good" party and an "anti" party juxtaposed. That happens in *Holiday,* too, where Katharine Hepburn gives an anti-party in her little bedroom upstairs while a stuffy party with rich people is going on downstairs.

Are there any good parties in movies where nobody's humiliated?

JK: In Dickens's books you always had those nice, cozy parties where just a piece of chicken would be so wonderful, and you'd feel so happy for the people because they had something to eat. And I think the best Dickens-type party in American movies is in *Meet Me in St. Louis,* where Margaret O'Brien sneaks downstairs to the party her sister is giving. Margaret was an obnoxious little sister and at the same time an adorable one. So alive, so delicious. The Dickens kind of party is the warm kind you get from good, decent people who don't know about big cities, people who find the Old Testament shocking. In *Meet Me in St. Louis* the people are just clean and wholesome but not dull—they're young and full of hope and the future, and they believe that the food is going to be just as appetizing as it looks. And the girls are going to sing so well they could be on Broadway, only they're just in a normal American home. And they play charades and you watch them and remember how much you love that game. It's a film about nothing at all where the father says, "We're going to move to New York," and everybody becomes miserable until the father changes his mind at the end. These kids can take such strength from this family. And you figure that this is the last generation before everything started to go downhill.

DL: John Ford had frontier parties, like the dance in *My Darling Clementine* on the wooden floor of the half-built church, the wedding party at the end of *The Searchers,* the cavalry dance in *She Wore a Yellow Ribbon.* These parties are emblems of civilization, optimistic signs of community—of order and peace in the middle of chaos. It's the classic, very old-fashioned notion of the party as a place to celebrate, as opposed to all the modern neurotic parties we've been talking about. Ford's parties are acts of strength in hostile environments where it takes courage to forget violence and war and just get all together and have sweetness and grace.

On at the party for the thousandth guest star on *The Love Boat.* Andy with camera, Robert Guillaume, Alexis Smith, June Allyson, Loretta Swit, Ginger Rogers, Doug Cramer, Lana Turner, Aaron Spelling, Mary Martin, Michele Lee, Cloris Leachman, Tom Bosley, and Carol Channing.

Reed

REED

When you're walking down streets like Sunset or Santa Monica Boulevards, there are lots of vending machines with different sex newspapers inside, and the papers always look like they've been sitting there forever, but you don't personally know anybody who puts ads in them or even buys them. Well, one night while I was sitting in a bar on Mulberry and Spring streets in New York with screenwriter Peter Koper, his wife, Gina, and two artists, Nick Ghiz and Joe Lewis, a young kid from L.A. named Reed sat down and told us how he'd lost his virginity at a swingers-type orgy in the Hollywood Hills.

When did it happen?

A couple of months ago. I was eighteen and I was dating this Rumanian girl. A lot of Rumanians have shown up in L.A. in the last ten years. More recently this girl has started prostituting herself, but before she was just a student nymphomaniac. I'm writing a novel, and she's in it a lot. She called me up this one night and said, "Ooo, I have dis party to go to and I have no way of getting dere. Would you like to go with me?" She's sixteen years old, so I thought it would be like a high-school party. So I picked her up—she lives in East Hollywood with her parents—and drove up this real snaky road up on Sunset Plaza in L.A., in the mountains over the Strip, to this A-frame house that's I guess famous in Los Angeles for being an old orgy house, but I didn't know it. Red Christmas lights all over the place, Bee Gees music. She knocks on the door and says, "Is Marty there?" and this old, old guy opens up. He's balding, has wire-rim glasses on, and his T-shirt says "Let's Boogie" across it. And I was a virgin, right? And even though I'd gone to high schools in L.A.—voluntary busing—and I'd always heard about the Hollywood swingers scene, I thought it was a fantasy. But here it was in front of me—and a heavy scene, too. The place was adorned in plastic palm trees and plastic fruits, and everybody was walking around in lingerie. Old, old women. I mean sixty years old, some of them.

Ruben Blades and actress Dolly Fox

Steve Rubell, Catherine Oxenberg, and Jelly Bean Benitez

Filmmaker John Waters and Peter Koper

Are you serious?

I found out later it was thirty dollars to get in and that this Marty had picked up the tab for me. So Maria walks over to this Marty, and sitting next to him is this gorgeous, voluptuous twenty-year-old creature who was mind-shatteringly beautiful. We exchange the usual pleasantries, but this girl, Dana, turns out to be a real bitter bitch, a real scag. And Marty says, "Well, I guess I'll show Maria around," and whips her off. So they're gone and I'm sitting there with Dana, trying to look inconspicuous while all these old ladies are looking at me, and I realize they think I'm the new piece of flesh. Some men were walking around bare-ass, but the women were in lingerie and this luscious but bitter girl was sitting there in a garter belt with stockings and nothing else. I'm like drooling over her,

but she doesn't really talk to me, so I snag one of her cigarettes and smoke it and then she takes me into this room where people are watching porno films and it's real bad juju in there, people all mean and bored with their lives. So we go on the balcony, where naked people are getting in and out of a hot tub. And then we walked over to the catered food section, which was all deli, and I was horrified by this big bowl of mayonnaise because it had a film over it and it was glowing in the red light. Then we walked into an area of cubbyholes with mattresses and she looks at me and says, "Take off your clothes." By this point I'm not even excited because the whole scene there really freaked me out and I had no desire to sleep with her. Call me a fag but I thought she was a bitch. However, I realized I couldn't live with myself if I

stormed out of there scared. And I realized it was great material for my career as a novelist. So I took off my clothes and folded them and I looked around and there was Maria—my nubile sort-of girlfriend giving Marty a blowjob, and that was depressing. We crawled into the same bed with them, and actually, my big concern was that Marty would want a homosexual encounter. But he didn't lay a finger on me. In fact, I think he was afraid of *me* coming on to him. He stayed his distance. By this time Dana is naked and I don't know what to do. I'm lying there trying to look relaxed, like "Mmmm, interesting scene." Dana realizes I'm not motivated and starts stroking my arm and I start making out with her but I'm totally impotent, and there's Marty next to me, grunting, a real contortionist, legs up around

Band leader Paul Shafer and Christopher Reeve at the Hard Rock Cafe

the shoulder, all these snazzy maneuvers. Finally I'm able to get a little aroused by her because I'm pretending she's my ex-girlfriend who I'd never had sex with, but I was very amateurish and she was losing patience. I never felt a thing. It was a blur. I didn't feel myself come or anything: I just knew it was finished. Then I rolled over and acted wiped out—although I had barely moved. Then Maria comes over to me, smiling, and spits Marty all over my face. I was repulsed beyond all imagination. I jumped up and ran across the house naked. I didn't care anymore. Horrible. What a way to lose it, you know. This was a few months ago.

Have you done it again since then?

Yes. The second time was more traditional—we had sex and I kicked her out afterward.

LAS VEGAS PARTIES

TV personality/musical director Paul Shaffer spends as much time as he can in Las Vegas. Paul reports:

"An ideal Vegas party would include Ray "Boom Boom" Mancini. And a nice touch would be a few managers putting down their own clients. I went to one recently that had both these elements. A few feet away from me was Boom Boom, and then across the room was a kind of comedian-impressionist—like a poor man's Fred Travalena. A guy nudges me and introduces himself, says, 'I love you on the Letterman show.' He tells me his name and says, 'I manage————.' He points across the room, tells me his client's name, and as he does, he lowers his glasses on his nose, looks over them, and gives me this 'look' of the most extreme disdain for his

client. The guy's own *manager* does this! That stayed with me."

BALTIMORE PARTIES

When I heard that John Waters was about to throw a fortieth birthday party for himself at an old-age home, I went down to Soho to ask him about it. He'd come up from Baltimore to give a lecture at NYU and was visiting at Peter and Gina Koper's loft—he had been best man at their wedding. Peter's a writer (he also produced John's movie Polyester) who went to school in Baltimore, and Gina's a designer who grew up there.

JW: Yes, I'm having my fortieth birthday party at an old-age home in Baltimore, The Waxter Center. The invitation's going to have a walker on it—my friend Ken Ingels is drawing it up for me. I'm admit-

119

ting to forty in a big way because all year long while you're thirty-nine people think you're lying anyway, so why not?

Where else have you had parties in Baltimore?

PK: Our wedding was in a pier we rented from the city for fifty dollars. And John gave me a bachelor party.

JW: I rented a school bus and we went to every low strip joint in Baltimore.

Are there any high strip joints?

JW: In Paris, maybe. Certainly not in Baltimore. The basic look is girls with dirty bare feet and tattoos. It took all night. And the bus! I felt like we were on the People's Temple bus riding to Jonestown for some Kool-Aid. No shocks. Like Guatemalan peasants could bring their chickens on with them. I think it must have been the bus that black religious groups rent, because there was a gospel robe left on one of the seats. It took all night, including a male strip joint—we were liberal.

PK: Remember that guy was bouncing his balls on my head?

JW: By that time he could've bounced *anything* on your head and you wouldn't have cared.

Was Peter's the only bachelor party you ever gave?

JW: No, but we always do the same thing because we all love those strip joints, so anything's a good excuse.

Was there ever a party you were dying to go to but you weren't invited?

JW: Let's see. . . . When I was a teenager I read about Truman Capote's ball and of course I wanted to go, but it wasn't likely since I was fourteen and in Baltimore. No, I guess I was seventeen. Anyway, I was in Baltimore. Was it sixty-four?

If you'd gone, it probably would've changed your life. Whatever happens to you in high school really affects you.

JW: I disagree. High school was not a big trauma for me—it was just boring. I wish I'd quit school in the

Max Van Peebles and screenwriter Desmond Nakano

120

Jacqueline Bisset and Hollywood
columnist George Christy

sixth grade—that way I would've made three more movies. I didn't learn a thing in school. I'd sit there in Catholic school reading the *Hundred Twenty Days of Sodom* by the Marquis de Sade and the nuns thought it was great—they didn't know what it was—because I was "reading" instead of "talking."

Did you have parties in high school?

JW: Yes! We'd crash so many. We'd appear with fifty people, go in, drink all the parents' liquor, and get arrested. This happened over and over, and my parents finally got so tired of coming to the police station, they said, "You can have parties at home." So that era started, but it only lasted through two parties, because my parents would sit trembling in their bedroom as everyone in the house got dead drunk and they figured, well, that this liberal method was not such a good way to handle the problem, either. I felt bad for my parents. I put them through such hell. I never said anything, of course, but I felt pangs. And we went to lots of parties where the girl would purposely get a job as somebody's babysitter just to be able to have a party there—a one-shot deal. When the police came we would dive through the windows. I put a scene sort of like that in *Desperate Living*—the parents came home and flipped out.

When did you get your first tuxedo?

JW: My mother curls her lip if you use that word. I bought my first "dinner jacket" just five or six years ago. Before that I would sometimes rent, or get them at thrift shops. I'd wear Levi's and a dinner jacket, that kind of stuff. For my high-school prom I went and rented the most hideous James Brown tuxedo that was leopard and stuff, and I never returned it. I still have it. I stole it. I'd given a fake name, so it was premeditated. And a few months later my mother saw it and was so pissed off—"What's that thing still doing in your closet?"

You got kicked out of NYU in the

Pia Zadora

George Maharis

Sixties for smoking pot. Had you smoked any at parties in high school?

JW: Yes. My parents used to drive me to this bar called Marticks, which was the beatnik bar in Baltimore. They didn't know what I was doing there—I guess they thought I'd meet someone intelligent there, I don't know. Even though legally I was under age to go in. But we'd stand outside. We called it the Jungle au Go Go. The owner knew we weren't twenty-one, but he liked us because we made these movies. I went through a whole period of hanging out with black people—"checkerboard parties."

That's cute. How were black parties different from your own parties?

JW: They were better. Cooler. At least I thought so. I was one of the few white people there.

And you didn't feel uncomfortable?

JW: Not then. I probably would now. I was a beatnik and that was part of it. During that period I met people who smoked pot. I had always made speeches about how I would never ever smoke pot. And then, the first second it was offered to me I said yes and I grabbed it. And I took acid in sixty-four in high school, before it was illegal, even. We got it from Shepherd Pratt Hospital. Sandoz acid, the original kind. I don't take anything now.

When you go all around the country giving lectures at colleges, do they have parties for you?

JW: They'll always have *something* for you afterward, even if they just take you out for a drink in a bar. To me they usually say, "We've got someplace you've got to see." Now I know what that place will be like, I *know* that "local color," but I go. I went to this one party once and it stands out in my mind: It was at this student's house and they had—absolutely nothing. Not the most rudimental party offering. No drinks, no soda—not even a potato chip. Not on purpose or anything. I guess they just weren't that experienced at party-giving and they sort

Paloma Picasso

of forgot that you have to have *some-thing*. A cigarette! *Something!* And the TV was on. But I sort of liked it because it was so ridiculous.

Is liquor necessary at parties?

JW: I'll say yes.—But wait. I have been to good parties with no liquor. In prison. Because I teach a film course in prison and there's a Christmas party with the convicts and their families, and it's nice. You get invitations from the prison—it's what you might call a severe theme party—and you have to RSVP and everything.

Is it minimum security?

JW: Maximum. My classes are murderers. It's only for people on the "fourth level," which means they're doing the best time. I even took a date.

How do you handle crashers at parties you give?

JW: I have a guard who pistol-whips with no witnesses. I give him a list with names. Once this girl came with her goddamn mother and she said, "But this is my *mother*," and I said, "Well, so what? You weren't even invited yourself." And once someone handed me a pres-ent and I *took* it and *then* kicked her out. Because of the humiliation she was causing me of *having* to kick her out.

John, this is harsh.

JW: But I don't *want* them there! I use a bouncer who looks like a bouncer but doesn't have the mind of one. He won't punch you out, but he looks like he will. I live in a high-rise and he stays downstairs at the outside door so they never even make it upstairs.

Are you insured in case he punches anybody?

JW: I have home insurance. Would that cover it?

I don't think so.

PARIS PARTIES

Fashion designer Larissa makes a few trips to Paris every year, usually during the collections, and she compared New York and Paris entertaining attitudes.

Peter Beard

Kelly LeBrock

Barbara Allen and Whitney Tower, Jr.

It was Franco Rossellini who introduced me to Imelda Marcos in the seventies. A few months after the Marcoses fled to Hawaii, while the newspapers were full of all the shoe stories, I asked him to tell me about the parties he'd gone to at the Malacanang Palace in Manila.

"She's a unique personality, Imelda. Adorable. I haven't seen her since three months before all this happened, and now with all these problems, I am surprised to see the lack of touch with reality that they had. But you know what is the most ironic thing? Three thousand pairs of shoes, it's not so rich *(laughs)*. Listen, I could tell you names of people with twenty thousand! I tell you the truth! When I heard 'three thousand pairs of shoes,' I thought to myself, Okay, maybe in *that drawer* she has three thousand, but I know Imelda, and she must have more stashed away—otherwise she would not be up to my expectations. In fact, I'm going to call her tomorrow in Honolulu because I just last night got the phone number, and I'll tell her, 'Listen, I'm dying to count the shoes, because I know you're hiding some.' You see, I think she must have left what she felt was a suitable amount that wouldn't shock people. 'Three thousand won't bother them . . .' You know? Imelda Marcos is a person of great charm, but they lost touch with political reality. I'm sure they were badly advised. I was to visit so many times at Malacanang. The parties were official parties, heads of state were coming . . . I was there when the pope was there, and when they opened the Heart Center. These parties were not 'luxurious.' They were very simple, very cozy, and a little, well, naïve. They wanted to show that they had five cakes instead of one, or more champagne than is needed. Just to be nice. It was not showing off—it was just a naïve way to entertain.

People in America live so poorly compared with the rich Europeans. Here they never hear of a butler or a maître d'hôtel. In Europe we all have a lot of staff in the houses, so

Literary agent Swifty Lazar and music-business legend Ahmet Ertegun

"The invitation situation is very different in Paris from New York. When people are in New York from Paris and I am invited to a party, I always say, 'Why don't you come along to this party with me?' Because I am sure the host or hostess will be delighted to meet them. Unless it's a sit-down dinner, and then of course you call in advance. But usually the host or hostess won't even ask anything more than perhaps, 'What is his name?' There won't be any investigating questions, because if they invited you, they trust you to have the good sense and good taste to bring somebody who won't shame you. But in Paris, the same people who you took to a *hundred* parties in New York will be very, very reluctant to mention that there's anyplace they

even *could* bring you—they don't even want to bring it up to the hostess because it will be a barrage of questions: 'Who is she? What does she do? Where does she come from? What is her pedigree?' A whole number!"

I asked Larissa why she thought there were more costume parties in Europe than in New York.

"In Europe they don't really work nine to five the way we do here. Those girls can sit at home for three weeks and whip together something with their friends, do a real production. It's so much work that, here in New York where our workdays are long, unless you are a transvestite and used to it, it's just too much trouble."

when they say things like, 'Mrs. Marcos had perfumes all over the bathrooms,' I say, 'Yes, every guest had a marvelous bathroom—exactly like the one I have at home—and yes, there were a lot of perfumes in these bathrooms, but only because she would receive from companies samples and, truthfully, I would never use any of them because they were from cheap companies that you would never buy.' And you know, Imelda's invitations were always very simple. Darling, if I showed you the invitation from the Queen of Thailand where we spent the week, I mean, it was a big thing in silk, all engraved in gold, and the special printing cost a fortune. The Marcoses never did anything like that. People have no understanding of what luxurious living is really like, so they are easily shocked. But let's be practical—the political situation in the Philippines is much more important to be thinking about than the consumption extravaganza, which was not so extravagant, anyway."

Joe Lewis is an artist and world traveler. He reminisced about a trip to Manila in 1975.

"I heard that Don King Enterprises was looking for an official photographer to go to Manila with all the players for the National Basketball Association's invitational tournament in the Philippines. I applied for the job, got hired, went out and bought my first camera, and pretty soon I was sitting on a plane to Manila reading the instruction booklet. When we got to the hotel there was a big press conference. Reporters were asking the players questions, and they had just finished laying out all the food on the buffet tables in the back when in storms two hundred Filipino whores with Mama-san yelling, 'All clean, all clean! Have papers!' Those girls descended on that buffet table and when they finally backed off there was nothing left but memories. Walt Frazier's going, 'Yes, well, uh, I like my outside shots . . .'

And the girls are eating like crazy. There was media coverage of the whole thing, too. I'll tell you, they didn't need their 'official photographer' that afternoon, because there wasn't a pack of Polaroid film left in the whole hotel—all the players were using it in their rooms."

Franco Rossellini reading his invitation from the Queen of Thailand

Weddings Funerals, Art Openings, Charities, Etc.

WEDDINGS

I wasn't invited to Madonna's wedding, but one of her best friends, Martin, knew I wanted to go so badly that he invited me as his date. We went out to L.A. with Keith Haring, checked into the Bel Air, and waited for the secret instructions to the secret location of the ceremony. It turned out to be at a house on a cliff in Malibu, and the guy who was letting them use it had just put it up for sale for six million dollars, so I realized that the wedding was actually an ad for the house—it would be "the house Madonna got married in."

It was just a family-type wedding. Keith talked to Sean's grand- mother, who was taking art classes, she said, at a senior citizens' center. And of course the helicopters swooped in, *Apocalypse Now*–style, and took telephoto pictures. Later in the papers it was easy to pick out Cher and me in these aerial shots because of our hair.

It was understood that it wouldn't be cool to take pictures since secrecy and privacy seemed to be the big themes of the event, so I didn't so much as take my camera out until we were leaving, and the only picture I snapped all day was one of Tom Cruise—when he jumped into our limo trying to get away from the photographers, I photographed him.

Sandro Chia wearing his nametag . . .
. . . at a party given to call attention to Senator Teddy Kennedy's pro-artist legislation

FUNERALS

Going to funerals is a good way to remember who's dead. I try to avoid funerals, but if you don't go to them it's easy to forget who's in heaven—acquaintances die and three months later I'm back to asking people how they are.

The whole idea of funeral parlors is probably a new idea when you think about it. I guess when people started living in apartments and didn't have much space, it was too shocking to put the body on the dining-room table. But nowadays nobody sees anything real, nobody faces anything. *I* certainly don't. People never see all the animals slaughtered for the meat they're eating.

Forgetting names is always bad, but it's terrible at funerals when people forget the name. What could be sadder? Or sometimes they just mispronounce it in the eulogy a hundred times, and each time it's so embarrassing, and it's so easy to prevent with a little care.

The most memorable thing for me during an around-the-world trip that I took once was walking along a trail in Bali and finding a bunch of people having a big happy party, and it turned out their friend had died and they were so thrilled for him that he was now having his next life.

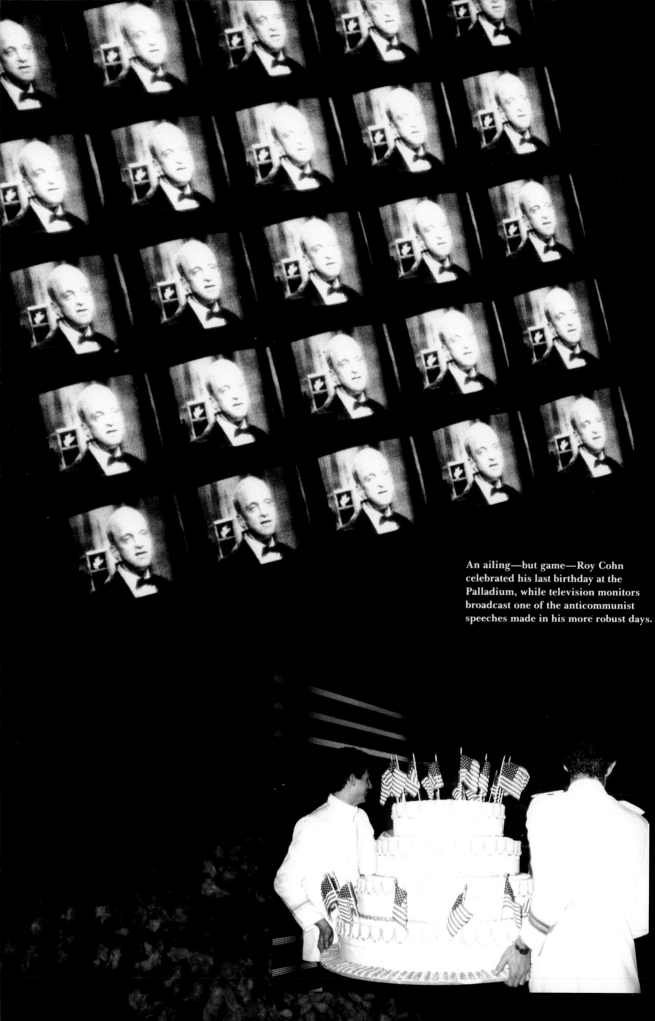

An ailing—but game—Roy Cohn celebrated his last birthday at the Palladium, while television monitors broadcast one of the anticommunist speeches made in his more robust days.

Victor Bockris and Ronnie Cutrone

Jean-Michel Basquiat

Keith Haring

Artist Ronnie Cutrone told me that Anna Magnani's funeral had a similar feeling, that it was the best party he ever went to:

"It was 1972 in Rome. Daniella Morera said, 'Come, dahdl-ling. We must not miss this.' It was right out of *La Dolce Vita*—men in black mohair suits and crisp white handkerchiefs rubbing tears out from under their dark sunglasses, and all these incredibly beautiful Italian women just dressed to the hilt. People were hanging out of their windows and off monuments. I went into the church and took a rose off her coffin and put it in my diary. Everyone was basically sad, but not completely, because they were all Catholics, so they knew she'd gone straight up to heaven and was already with the Blessed Virgin."

ART OPENINGS

Keith Haring is an artist whose roots are in parties, but at the opening he describes below, the ultimate dinner party nightmare came true—you walk into your own party and wonder, "Where's the food?" and you're told, "What food? We thought you were bringing the food." Keith says:

"I was having an opening at Leo Castelli's gallery and then a big elegant dinner at the Palladium afterward—we'd silkscreened these really beautiful invitations. I was late leaving my place for the gallery, and I went down in my elevator and it got stuck. First time in my life, stuck in the elevator. So I climbed out into the shaft through the hole in the top, finally made it out. Got to the opening and on the way into the gallery, somebody throws tar and feathers at me. My father shoved me out of the way. I thought this was a gun or a bomb they were pulling out of this bag because everyone just jumped back out of the way. And then they threw feathers everywhere so no one could see anything, and then they ran away, and no one ran after them or anything because it happened so fast everyone was all in shock. I guess it was an art statement. The tar mostly hit my friend Joey Dietrich, who's a model, so he has a great body and it looked terrific, like a Bruce Weber

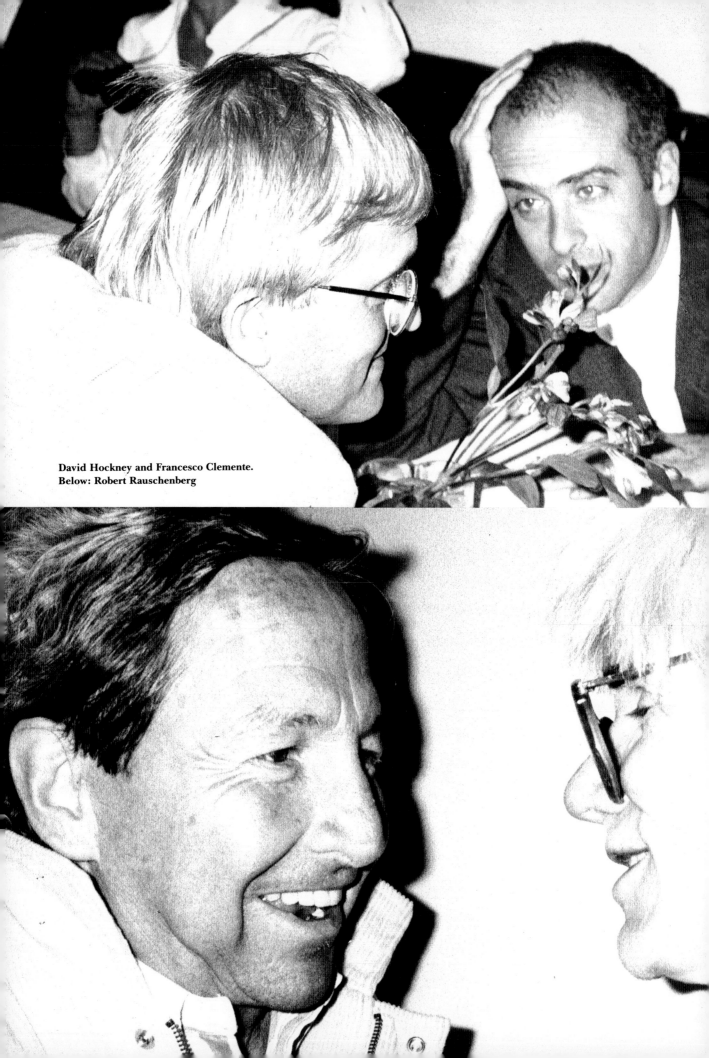

David Hockney and Francesco Clemente.
Below: Robert Rauschenberg

Julian Schnabel

Peter McDermott of the painting team
"Messrs. McDermott & McGough,
Painters of Pictures"

Liza Minnelli, Halston, and Martha Graham

photograph—he had to rip off his T-shirt and he had tar all over his chest. My father was trying to clean it off with turpentine. I did get a little on me, so I go and get cleaned up and then I tell everybody, 'Just be normal, don't ask me about it.' About six o'clock somebody tells me, 'You're going to freak out, but I just called the Palladium and asked them how the dinner was coming along, and they don't know anything about the caterer—there's no food there.' The dinner's supposed to start at eight. We had agreed on a really good caterer and somehow they assumed I had contacted them and I thought they had, and eventually I guess Rudolf took the blame for the mix-up and he ran out to a deli and got cold cuts and roast beef and we were eating on paper plates and things. It was *so* embarrassing. But actually it turned out okay, because not one single celebrity I invited showed up, so it was just my friends, and they understood. Plus, to compensate, Rudolf kept giving us free bottles of Dom Perignon, so nobody cared because we just got drunk. But we were all starving, and I left there, drunk, went home, got some sleep, got up at four A.M. and went to The Garage and that was fun, the best time to go, a really serious dancing place. It opens around midnight, but it's not really fun until six o'clock."

Ronnie Cutrone contrasts art openings in the Eighties with those in the Sixties and Seventies:

"At one time you'd have an opening and there'd be fifty to a hundred people there, and then afterward there would usually be a party given for the artist by somebody, or else the artist would give one himself. But in the Eighties, the opening itself *was* the party. Keith Haring and I convinced Tony Shafrazzi—and he liked the idea himself—to make the openings at his gallery more of an event. We wanted to make them more palatable to the masses, because people don't just go to an opening to look at art—they go to pick up their next girlfriend or boyfriend, to find love

Glenn O'Brien and David Johansen/
Buster Poindexter between sets

Publisher/author Dennis Smith
surrounded by Carina Anderson and his
sons Brendan, Sean, and Dennis.

Wedding day in Massachusetts for Maria
Shriver and Arnold Schwarzenegger

Maria and Arnold with cake on his hands

Grace Jones grooming herself in the plane en route to the wedding

Wedding cake in a wheelchair on Park Avenue

and drinks and sex and music—but the stuff on the walls makes a great environment to have this good time in. So I always made great tapes and we had a good sound system in the gallery—decent one, anyway. It got to the point where there were over three thousand people at my opening in eighty-five. The whole street outside the gallery was mobbed. This kind of event shattered the barrier of an art opening being exclusive. But the funny thing was, even though people were at this big party with all this food and booze and fashion and music, they still had the mentality that was expecting there to be another party—the 'real' party—later on. They'd be asking you, 'Where's the party going to be?' And you'd tell them, '*This* is the party. You're *in* it.' But they wouldn't believe you."

Mr. Chow wishing and blowing

141

Sam Bolton, Angie Dickinson, and Harry Reasoner at a Julio Iglesias performance

Senator Ted Kennedy

CHARITIES

Charity balls give people a chance to get dressed up and put on their jewelry. It's nice to see a woman who's "groomed"—who has "that" hair and "those" little bangs.

Each charity seems to have its own circle of people who get involved with it. Whoever chairs the event sets the tone. And then you have tribes of people who follow different charities.

Americans give 2.5 percent of their income to charity, according to a recent Rockefeller Fund study. In Europe the whole point of being rich is to have more money than other people and you're not supposed to give it away, but for Americans, the charity parties are a very good way to let people feel pious, and by adjusting the price of admission to the charity "event," you control the status of the people who go to them. They can make themselves part of a group they might not otherwise be a part of. It's a way of buying into culture. Americans don't have a rigidly defined social structure, so you can make it big here by giving charity parties. Obviously, it's all for good causes, but if at the head of somebody's table was going to be her hairdresser's shampoo assistant, for example, she wouldn't pay the amount of money she would if it were going to be Jackie Onassis.

And it's nice, too, the little things they give you on the tables, the favors—the lipsticks and perfume. And you never know too many of the people at these balls, so you're not obligated to stand around and go, "Ooh, ooh, darling, mmm, mmm." Watching these people in action is kind of elegant, too.

These big balls cost a lot to produce, so if you're involved in running them, it's hard to figure out how much to spend, because while you don't want to cut into the proceeds that go to the charity, you do want people to come back the next year—you don't want them to feel like they've been to a cheap event. Professional party designers like Renny Reynolds organize really spectacular events like the Metropolitan Museum of Art things, and fund-raisers for the School of

Architect Peter Marino gave his West Highland terrier Ziggy a birthday party

American Ballet, where the donations are as high as ten thousand dollars per table. "We may take a fee of twenty to forty thousand for planning a large-scale party," he says, "but when you'll be netting several hundred thousand dollars, it's worthwhile to do something the party-goer will remember and circle on their calendar for the *next* year, too." Renny offers the big dance that the New York Public Library has every year as a good example of how to plan an event: "The hundred or so Friends of the Library give private dinners at their

homes before the event, and they make sure that the people who come to their house are giving their five-hundred-dollar or whatever-it-is contribution to the library, and then after dinner everyone goes to the library for the dance. That way the library doesn't get into the cost of the food, and still people are focused on the cause, because they're right in the library dancing. That's an extremely bright way of raising money."

With her signature European accent, Aline Franzen is a unique personality

who is involved with more charities than anyone I've ever met:

How did you get so involved with charities?

I had charity at home: My mother was always doing charity since I was a little girl and she told me I must help other people. Unfortunately, I'm called the Queen of Charity in New York, Washington, and Los Angeles—"unfortunately," because every charity is after me— "Mrs. Franzen, will you help us?"— and yet I am only one and I cannot help hundreds of charities. This

"Queen of Charity" Aline Franzen

year I did already three. I was chairman of the Princess Grace Foundation and now I'm chairman for the Boys Town. I don't have children, therefore I am helping. Since twenty-two years I am helping Boys Town of Italy.

If people didn't have the expense of big charity balls—if they just sent letters to people asking for money—do you think you would raise more? I mean, they wouldn't have to lay out money for the hotel, the waiters, the food, the flowers, the music . . .

Forget about it! People would not send the money. They like to get dressed up in jewels and beautiful clothes. All my charities are formal, except if I do a cocktail or a luncheon. And we give people a lot for their money—the show, the food, the little gifts to take home— and you help the worthy cause. Always there's a raffle, always door prizes. People like our door prizes.

What's the most important part of planning an event?

The committee. To have celebrities and people known. If you send

a letter with names of unknown people, people don't open their antennas.

When you have celebrities on the committee, do they have to work?

No. To give their names is enough. With stars it's very difficult. Four or five months ago Telly Savalas was coming to a benefit. In the last moment he got a commercial for the Ford. So what can I tell him? "Don't do the commercial, Telly—come and help me?" Of course not. I understand. Telly is a very old friend who always tries to

145

Artist Arman and his wife Corice

Daniela Morera, Richard Berstein, and
Marc Balet

help me. I met him fourteen years ago when he accepted to be my co-chairman for the Industrial Home for the Blind, because his grandmother had problems with her eyes.

What are some of the charities you've done events for?

Meals on Wheels, UNICEF, I don't know how many times I was chairman for USO, Greek Orthodox charities, One to One—you remember the retarded home and Geraldo Rivera with the children chained? Willowbrook? I did that one. I did the Bicentennial for the Brooklyn Museum, Actors Studio, Odyssey House, Save the Children, the Italian Earthquake twice, Bide-a-Wee Animal Homes I'm doing all the time—I have lunches, I sold a cat and a dog . . .

What about the medical charities?

Dahling, I did every disease. Every one. I raised over half a million for the American Heart Association. I did the American Cancer Society in Orlando. I did the Kidney Foundation, National Hemophiliac, Fight for Sight, Muscular Dystrophy. It doesn't exist that I don't help. So long as people exist, charity will exist. Because it is the only way you can help people.

SHOOTING PARTIES

In the U.S. we hear more about shooting sprees than shooting parties, and I didn't know much about those long glamorous weekends when you get invited to somebody's plantation or country estate and go on forays every morning and afternoon to kill creatures that live on their land or fly in their airspace. People say that at one time the best shoots were here in America. Prince Kyril Scherbatow had gone on shooting parties all over Europe and America and he told me what they were like in the thirties.

"The best shoots were in South Carolina. Fabulous dove shoots outside of Charleston at Adam's Run, the place of Barbara Hutton's fa-ther. Inland was dove and quail; closer to the water was duck. You'd stay on the plantation. Some would stay outside because there was no room, but you always had ten to fifteen people at the house during shooting times—people would come for long weekends, lots of dinners and parties.

"I used to shoot at a place called Arcadia—thirty-three thousand acres in Georgia that belonged to George Vanderbilt. It was the greatest duck shooting you've ever seen. There was so much vermin that there wasn't a possibility of shooting anything else. Ducks, deer, and wild boar. These were domestic pigs gone wild let's say a hundred years before. And boy, they were ferocious. They became like razorbacks. To hunt these you needed what they call 'hog dogs.' The next plantation over from Vanderbilt's was Bernard Baruch's. Baruch was away so I asked his overseer if I could borrow a hog dog and he said yes, he'd loan me one. I was using a Mauser rifle. The dog was really good. We cornered that hog—I saw him in the swamp and there was water up to 'here' and trees fallen down, and I was thinking I'd get bitten by one of those water moccasins. I aimed and shot at the hog. The bullet went through its neck and killed the hog, but it kept on going and killed the dog on the other side of him, too. The dog lay there dead and I was in despair.

"I went back and discussed it with George Vanderbilt and we agreed that I should get Baruch another one. Those dogs were specially trained in Kentucky and we called and the price was very high for then—about five hundred dollars. So the dog was delivered to the overseer and he called me and said he'd better try him out to make sure he was good, so that I could return him and get another if he wasn't. The overseer started to work with him and somehow this dog jumped and somehow he accidentally shot him. So with one dog dead and one wounded, I decided to call it quits. I had tried. Anyway, Baruch himself didn't shoot."

C.Z. Guest

Mariel Hemingway

Parting Thou

Goethe said somewhere that the trouble with parties is that they use up all the energy that could be used for doing something else, and that if you don't do the "something else," you won't have anything real to celebrate at the next party. Jane Austen, on the other hand, pointed out that "everything happens at parties!" The great party-giver Elsa Maxwell took a position somewhere between those two when she admitted that giving parties was a "trivial avocation," but that it paid the dues for her "union card in humanity."

The thing about parties is, once you start, you just want more. It's like occupying a foreign country—you've got to be there all the time or it'll slip away from you. But it's also like a bad relationship—if you ever stop it, it feels so good when you do that you find out how bad it really was.

I don't have a dream party in my mind that I'd want to go to. And anyway, it's like "answered prayers" —if I had a dream party, and if I ever actually got invited to it, it'd probably be a bomb.

The crowd outside St. Patrick's after the memorial mass for Andy. Opposite: The wall lining the staircase on the way to the lunch at the Diamond Horseshoe

Coda

The lunch at the Diamond Horseshoe following the memorial mass was the most atypical "Andy Warhol party" anyone had ever been to—no crashers, and no Andy. All the different phases and facets of his life came together, from his relatives up from Pittsburgh to Timothy Leary and Viva, from Don Johnson to Philip Johnson to Jed Johnson, from Dominique De-Menil to Raquel Welch. People looked around and realized the impact Andy had had on their lives: Who could Lou Reed and Ann Bass ever have in common except Andy? Where else could Claus Von Bülow hug Debby Harry?

Andy once said, "People think that everyone who came to the Factory was there because of me, that I was some kind of big attraction, but that's backwards—I was the one who was hanging around everybody else. I just paid the rent, and the great people came just because the door was open. They weren't coming to see me, they came to see each other. They came to see who came."

By going out night after night to every event he could, Andy gave everybody else something to go out for—the chance to have fun seeing him. On the day of his memorial, people did turn up to see each other, that's true, but there was the overwhelming feeling that it was affection for Andy more than anything else that had moved them all to come. It was a party that seemed to bring out the best in everyone.

PH

Chris Stein and Debbie Harry

Wilfredo Rosado and Pat Ast

**Underground figures from the 60s—
Taylor Mead and Gerard Malanga**

Yoko Ono and Grace Jones

Art critic John Richardson and Boaz
Mazor

Fred Hughes and Keith Haring

Bianca Jagger

Richard E. Berlin, Jr., and Jay Shriver

Paul Morrissey, 60s
Factory Foto-grapher
Billy Name, and 60s
"superstar" Ultra Violet

Richard Gere and artist Francesco Clemente

Raquel Welch and Andre Weinfeld

Andy's brother John Warhola, his wife, Margaret, and their son Donald.

Jed Johnson and Catherine Jones

Andy's cousin Eugenia King with his
housekeepers Aurora and Nena Bugarin

Andre Balazs and Katie Ford Balazs

Actress Geraldine Smith, rock star Ric Ocasek, and journalist Liz Derringer

Sitting in front of Andy's *Last Supper* painting—Lisa Robinson, Fran Lebowitz, and Marc Balet

Liza Minnelli

Andy's nephew Paul Warhola and Paul's wife, Lorene.

Dominique de Menil

Halston

Stephen Mazoh, Katharine Johnson, and Dominick Dunne

Photo Credits

Page 9, *top*, Sam Bolton. Page 10, Paige Powell. Page 13, Paige Powell. Page 16, *bottom*, Paige Powell. Page 17, Pat Hackett. Page 19, Paige Powell. Pages 20–21, Paige Powell. Page 25, Paige Powell. Page 26, Paige Powell. Page 27, Paige Powell. Page 28, *top and bottom*, Paige Powell. Page 30, Pat Hackett. Page 31, *bottom*, Paige Powell. Page 36, *left*, Paige Powell; *right*, Edit de Ak. Page 37, *top and bottom*, Pat Hackett. Page 38, Pat Hackett. Page 39, Pat Hackett. Page 41, *top*, Paige Powell; *bottom*, Pat Hackett. Page 44, Pat Hackett. Page 45, Pat Hackett. Page 46, *top*, Pat Hackett. Page 47, *center*, Paige Powell; *bottom*, Jeffrey Slonim. Page 48, *left*, Pat Hackett. Pages 48–49, Pat Hackett. Page 49, *right*, Pat Hackett. Page 51, Pat Hackett. Page 53, *left*, Paige Powell. Page 54, Paige Powell. Page 55, *bottom left*, Pat Hackett. Page 57, Paige Powell. Pages 58–59, Pat Hackett. Page 60, *top*, Sam Bolton; *bottom*, Pat Hackett. Page 61, Paige Powell. Page 62, Pat Hackett. Page 64, *top and bottom*, Pat Hackett. Pages 66–67, Pat Hackett. Page 70, Pat Hackett. Page 74, *top and bottom*, Pat Hackett. Page 75, Paige Powell. Page 77, *top*, Pat Hackett. Page 79, Paige Powell. Pages 82–83, Pat Hackett. Pages 84–85, Pat Hackett. Pages 86–87, Pat Hackett. Page 88, Pat Hackett. Page 89, Sam Bolton. Page 90, *top*, Pat Hackett. Pages 90–91, Pat Hackett. Page 91, *top*, Pat Hackett. Page 94, Paige Powell. Page 95, *top and bottom*, Pat Hackett. Page 100, *top and bottom*, Paige Powell. Page 101, Pat Hackett. Page 109, Pat Hackett. Page 110, *bottom*, Pat Hackett. Page 112, *top and bottom*, Paige Powell. Pages 114–115, Pat Hackett. Page 116, Pat Hackett. Page 117, *top*, Pat Hackett. Page 118, Pat Hackett. Page 119, Pat Hackett. Page 120, Pat Hackett. Page 121, Paige Powell. Page 123, Pat Hackett. Page 127, Pat Hackett. Page 130, *top and bottom*, Pat Hackett. Page 131, Pat Hackett; *inset*, Pat Hackett. Page 132, *top*, Pat Hackett. Pages 134–135, *bottom*, Sam Bolton. Page 135, *top*, Paige Powell. Page 137, *top and bottom*, Pat Hackett. Page 142, *top and bottom*, Pat Hackett. Page 143, Sam Bolton. Pages 144–145, Pat Hackett. Page 145, *right*, C. J. Zumwalt. Page 146, *top*, Paige Powell. Pages 148–149, Paige Powell. Pages 150–151, Wilfredo Rosado. Page 151, Wilfredo Rosado. Page 152, *top and bottom*, Pat Hackett. Page 153, Pat Hackett. Page 154, *top left and bottom left*, Pat Hackett. Pages 154–155, *top*, Pat Hackett. Page 155, *top right*, Pat Hackett; *bottom*, Pat Hackett. Page 156, *top left*, Wilfredo Rosado; *top right*, Wilfredo Rosado; *bottom*, Sam Bolton. Page 157, *top*, Pat Hackett; *bottom left*, Pat Hackett; *bottom right*, Wilfredo Rosado. Page 158, *top*, Pat Hackett; *bottom left*, Sam Bolton. Page 159, *top left*, Pat Hackett. Pages 158–159, *bottom*, Pat Hackett. Page 159, *top right*, Pat Hackett. Page 159, *bottom right*, Pat Hackett.

All photos not credited are by Andy Warhol.

Thanks to

Paige Powell, for all her creative help.

Also,
Monica Ackerman, Glenn Albin, Steven M.L. Aronson, Scott Asin, Marc Balet, Sam Bolton, Robert Becker, Brigid Berlin, Remy Blumenthal, Roz Cole, Vincent Fremont, Patrick Fox, Lulu Hamlin, Brett Garwood, Joe Holland, Fred Hughes, Benjamin Liu, Zanne Lenow, Christopher Makos, Jane Trapnell Marino, Len Morgan, David Pawloski, Sharon Phair, Mark Pietrasanta, Rammel Z, Wilfredo Rosado, Kevin Sessums, Dorthea Tanning, Juliet Walker, Michael Walsh, Alan Wanzenberg, Jackie Weld.

At Crown Publishers,
Editors Pam Thomas and David Groff, Editor in Chief Betty A. Prashker, Director of Design Ken Sansone, Senior Publicist Susan Magrino, Erica Marcus, and Wilson Henley.